Seeking Happiness

Between Ignorance and Enlightenment VII

By
Venerable Master Hsing Yun

Translated by
Venerable Miao Hsi and Cherry Lai

© 2008 Buddha's Light Publishing

By Venerable Master Hsing Yun
Translated by Venerable Miao Hsi and Cherry Lai
Edited by Tom Manzo, Robin Stevens and Shujan Cheng
Cover and book designed by Mei-Chi Shih

Published by Buddha's Light Publishing
3456 S. Glenmark Drive,
Hacienda Heights, CA91745, U.S.A.
Tel: (626)923-5144/ (626)961-9697
Fax: (626)923-5145 / (626)369-1944
E-mail: itc@blia.org
Website: www.blpusa.com

ISBN: 978-1-932293-27-2

Library of Congress Cataloging-in-Publication Data

Xingyun, da shi.
  Seeking happiness / by Venerable Master Hsing Yun ; translated by Fo Guang Shan International Translation Center ; edited by Tom Manzo & Shujan Cheng.
      p. cm. -- (Between ignorance and enlightenment ; 7)
  Translation of selections from Chinese.
  ISBN 978-1-932293-27-2 (pbk. : alk. paper)
  1. Fo Guang Shan Buddhist Order--Doctrines. 2. Buddhism--Doctrines. 3. Religious life--Buddhism. I. Manzo, Tom. II. Cheng, Shujan. III. Fo Guang Shan International Translation Center. IV. Title. V. Series.

  BQ9800.F6392X55467 2008
  294.3'444--dc22

                                                          2008010474

Acknowledgements

*W*e received a lot of help from many people and we want to thank them for their efforts in making the publication of its book possible. We especially appreciate Venerable Tzu Jung, the Chief Executive of the Fo Guang Shan International Translation Center, Venerable Hui Chi, Abbot of Hsi Lai Temple, Venerable Yi Chao for their support and leadership; Venerable Miao Hsi and Cherry Lai for their translation; Tom Manzo, Shujan Cheng and Robin Stevens for their editing; Louvenia Ortega for her proofreading; Mei-Jane Cheng and Kevin Hsyeh, for preparing the manuscript for publication; and Mei-Chi Shih for her book and cover design. Our appreciation also goes to everyone who has supported this project from its conception to its completion.

Introduction

In every life experience, we are challenged to look at both the positive and the negative aspects of our surroundings, and to promote what is good and to diminish what is not. In these essays we see how a moment of thought can affect our state of mind and transform our lives.

A moment of thought may bring us a greater understanding of life so that we can see goodness in our world, maintain our physical and mental health, participate in the betterment of society and the world, and ultimately find happiness in everything we do.

These essays skillfully relate the natural world to our human existence and our existence as individuals to our role within society. The essays synthesize East and West, citing a Harvard University medical professor, various sutras, Confucius, and other great thinkers.

May each short essay provide you a moment to contemplate life, to help you look at life from a different perspective, and thus to find happiness in your life!

Tom Manzo, Ph. D.

CONTENTS

SEEKING HAPPINESS

We live life because of happiness. If life were only filled with suffering, it would be meaningless to live. As humans, we all have different goals in life due to our differing value systems. Some people want to make a lot of money, thinking it brings happiness. However, when there is too much money, it can bring much suffering. As the saying goes, "Humans die for money." What happiness, then, is wealth?

Some people believe that family is the source of happiness, but when family members do not get along with one another, what happiness is there in living with all the infighting? Others seek happiness in love and pursue it wholeheartedly. But when love and hate are twins, love can easily turn into hate, and the deeper the love, the worse the hate. When spouses and lovers have a falling out and sometimes become each other's worst enemies, it seems better to be single and unattached.

Those who are fond of power think that there is happiness within it. So they seek public office and run for high positions. However, many abuse their authority and end up being on the wrong side of the law. It seems that the higher they climb, the harder they fall, and high positions and power are not always the source of happiness.

Other people seek happiness in their careers. They open a factory here, a company there, or a conglomerate locally and another in a foreign country. They shoulder heavy responsibilities as they juggle their accounts and the balance sheet, and work with customers, suppliers, and employees. They become poor rich people; what happiness is there?

Other people retreat into the woods, high up in the mountains in their search for happiness. For them, happiness is the company of light breezes and the clear moon. Some look for a simple life and are happy with their lot, savoring the happiness of simplicity. Others enjoy reading, and as they bask in the ocean of books, they discover the way to settle their minds and the source of wisdom. They have found happiness in life.

Happiness also lies in peace, kind thoughts, the absence of

cravings, and contentment. While happiness is sought every-where, it is actually not anywhere but right inside the treasury of our hearts. Ask a bird why it flies in the sky and it will reply, "There is happiness in the sky!' Ask a fish why it swims in the water and it will answer, "There is happiness in the water!" Ask a lake why it flows amidst the mountains and it will explain, "There is happiness in the mountains!" When we ask people why they are always busy running about here and there, the response is, "By making broad connections in the world and benefiting humanity, there is happiness!"

Where is happiness? There is happiness in religion, cultiva-tion, serving others, and a calm mind. When we have heart and mind, happiness is right within!

TURN OR GO STRAIGHT

On the path of life, sometimes we need to go straight ahead and other times we have to make turns in order to reach our goals. If we do not turn around when we need to, we will not "see the other shore." But when we need to move ahead and do not, we will miss a prime opportunity. When we have to make a turn on the road of life, we have to decide whether to go right or left. We cannot make the wrong turn. And when we move ahead, we need to decide whether to move fast or slow, stay close or go far. Regrettably, some choose to make a turn when they should have moved straight ahead. Other times, people charge forward when they should have made a turn instead. Thus, they create many difficulties for themselves in life.

There are many examples in Chinese history where battles were lost and dynasties fell because emperors and generals failed to make the proper turn when required, or stopped when they should have charged ahead. As a result, they failed when they were within reach of success.

Of course, there were others who made all the right moves at the right times and gained an eminent place in history. Venerable Master Jianzhen attempted to travel to Japan seven times before he made it. He was undeterred by the first six failures. By forging ahead, he finally succeeded in bringing Buddhism and Chinese culture to Japan and was honored as the father of Japanese culture. Venerable Master Xuanzhuang went straight ahead on his path to India and was successful in bringing Buddhist sutras back to China. Sakyamuni Buddha was determined to achieve Buddhahood and finally reached his goal.

Confucius never intended to become an official. But he realized that the power of politics could help foster academics and education, and so was willing to take up a post in the imperial court. His story is illustrative of someone who knew how to make the right turns in life. We have witnessed the reunion of West and East Germany, and dialogue between the two Koreas after half a century of confrontation. Their governments know how to make turns.

On the battlefield, sometimes we need to charge bravely ahead. Other times we have to change our strategy. In opening a highway to the top of a mountain, we need to wind and turn around the slopes. We cannot go straight up, without winding and turning. In Taiwan, the highway from south to north goes straight up, while the one joining east to west is famous for its winds and turns.

As the saying goes, "There are many doors of convenience, but there is only one truth to reach for." Therefore, why should we be attached to any single path on the road of life as long as we reach our destination? When the road ahead is blocked, why not take a detour? Therefore, we need not be confrontational in our attitude toward others. Being stubborn and not giving an inch will not necessarily lead to victory. If we sail with the wind and make proper turns along the way, then the path of life will be smooth sailing.

THE WISE AND THE MEAN

There are many kinds of people: good, evil, kind and vicious. We encounter them as scholars, farmers, laborers, businessmen, soldiers, policemen, politicians and economists. They may be wise, foolish, moralistic or unethical, but generally they are either wise or mean.

Who are the wise and who are the mean? The wise are people who take joy in helping others achieve good deeds, while the mean aid others in devious acts. A wise person is open and shares with others. A mean person is secretive and does not share.

Humble Table, Wise Fare states, "The wise never harm others, and the mean never blame themselves. The mean blame others for their mistakes, and always complain about their fate and the people around them. In covering up their own shortcomings, their vice is actually more evident. The wise take the faults of others as their own responsibility and blame themselves. In reforming their ways, their morals improve everyday. We should stay away from the mean, but we should not openly be their enemies. We should get close to the wise, but we should not compromise ourselves."

The wise are usually open and honest, and the mean usually secretive and dishonest. This is the difference between the wise and the mean. Whether we want to be wise or mean depends on our vows and resolve. There are people who appear to be wise and who are actually mean, and vice versa. When the wise are our friends, they not only go through thick and thin with us but also help when we need them most. On the other hand, when the mean are our friends, they only flatter us when we are doing well. If we are down in life, they will not help us and will even take advantage of our situation. We all want to be with the wise, and distant from the mean. In relating to people in daily life, it is not difficult to figure out who they are.

When we make friends with the wise, the relationship is as clear as water, and because it is so clear, it lasts. With people who are mean, the relationship may seem as sweet as honey, but the sweetness wears off quickly. Confucianism teaches, "Being with the kind is like staying in an orchid garden. One gets used to the

fragrance and does not notice it. Being with the unkind is like being in a fish market. One gets used to the stench and is not repulsed by it." A relationship with the wise may take time to develop in the beginning, but it will bear good fruits in the end. Although it may be easy to start a friendship with a mean person, when he reveals his true character later we will suffer.

In conducting oneself and handling ones' affairs in society, there will be all kinds of benefits and losses. If we deal with the wise, the results will not be risky; if we deal with the mean, the results will be hard to predict.

The mean are always calculating like a scale. When we enjoy fame and fortune, they lower their heads to flatter us. When we are no longer doing well, they look down on us. They treat us like flowers, wearing us on their heads when we are in bloom and throwing us out and treating us like nothing when we wither.

How do we seek out the wise? We pay attention to character, morals, compassion and integrity. How do we avoid befriending the mean? When we see unethical, miserly, and hypocritical behavior, we know we are in the company of the mean. It is, therefore, not difficult to tell the wise from the mean, by distinguishing through morals and discipline.

THE DEVIL AND THE ANGEL

A painter once wanted to paint a portrait of Jesus Christ. So he traveled around the world in search of the perfect model with a beautiful and holy face, offering a large sum of money. After some time, he found a model and finished the portrait.

Years later, people began to tell the painter that he should also paint a portrait of the devil to display alongside the holiness seen in the portrait of Jesus Christ to illustrate the contrast between good and evil. The painter went off on another search for a model, only this time he looked for one with a vicious face. During his search he learned of a man in jail who had committed many heinous crimes and whose malicious looks were said to be just like those of the devil. After special arrangements were made with the prison, the painter was allowed to have the prisoner as his model.

In the process of his work, he found the prisoner familiar and discovered that he was the same model he had used for the portrait of Jesus! The prisoner eventually told him the reason for his downfall. After receiving the large modeling fee for the Jesus Christ portrait, he indulged in a life of decadence and spent his money quickly. Unable to take control of his life, he turned to crime and ended up in jail. The painter felt sorry for the prisoner after hearing his story and lamented the fact that humans could be both the holy and the devil.

There is a similar story in Buddhism. Once the Honorable Sariputra, the Buddha's disciple, met an old friend that he had not seen for a long time and was shocked to find that his old friend now looked evil. When asked why, his friend replied that he had been busy carving a statue of a vicious ghost. Sariputra explained that in visualizing the face of a wicked ghost during his work, his friend's looks changed with his thoughts and became just as vicious. Conversely, if he were to carve a statue of the Buddha, his mind would be filled with compassion and harmony. Then, both his thoughts and appearance would be beautiful. On hearing this, his friend switched to carving Buddha statues. After several years had passed, he began to look compassionate because his

thoughts had changed, and people were happy to be around him.

Since our faces reflect our minds, our thoughts create all forms and matters. The *Awakening of Faith in the Mahayana* speaks about "two gates of the mind:" the "gate of the true mind" is Buddha Nature, and the "gate of arising and ceasing thoughts" is the mind of humans. Both Buddha Nature and the human mind hinge on the same mind. There is the good of heaven and the evil of hell in the same mind. We do not know the number of times we rise to heaven and fall into hell in a day. We hold the ten dharma realms within our minds, and as humans, we hold the key to our rise and fall because above us are the realms of Buddha, bodhisattva, pratyekabuddha, and sravaka; and below us those of hell, hungry ghost, and animal.

If we relate to others with the Buddha mind in our human world, then the world changes into a Buddha world with us. If we relate to others with the devil's mind, then the world will become a living hell. Being the Buddha or the devil depends on the mind. What should our choice be? How, then, can we not be careful?

ADVANCING AND RETREATING

When we learn to drive, it is not enough for us just to learn to move forward. Knowing how to back up is just as crucial. When we learn to drive a boat, we cannot just go forward. It is also very important to know how to make turns and how to back it up. In life, we cannot charge full steam ahead all the time. Knowing how to advance and retreat is what we should cultivate in life.

If we simply charge ahead, what will happen if there is a wall in front of us? If you only know how to back up, what will you do if there is a cliff or pit behind you? We should only move forward and retreat when necessary. In doing so we can live reasonably.

When we encourage others, we often tell them to move forward, but we also need to realize that what we see in front of us is only half the world. There is another half behind us. Therefore, advancing is not good in and of itself, and retreating is not necessarily bad.

We should be able to move ahead in life as easily as we are able to back off. On the battlefield, it is important that troops charge forward courageously when they are winning. If they are losing and need to retreat, the results would be unthinkable if the general in charge is not a good strategist. It is easy to fight a winning battle but difficult to retreat when losing. So we should be good at advancing, and understand when and how to retreat.

The *Analects of Confucius* says, "A man of courage and fortitude who is successful and broad-minded, by looking ahead and behind, will benefit the world. However, if he is narrow-minded and focused on the path, he can only benefit himself." Before we charge forward or retreat, we must assess the situation. Is there still space ahead? How treacherous and dangerous is the road? If we retreat when we should not because there is no more room to advance, what should we do? The story "Not Retreating One Step," in the *One Hundred Parables Sutra*, serves as an excellent example for us, helping to teach us how to reassess when to progress and when to retreat.

Moving ahead and retreating when necessary is our duty in life. If we do not move ahead on our risk-filled journey and break the ice-logged river of life, how can we reach our goal? If we do not retreat when we need to in order to safeguard our last line of defense, how can we protect our bases?

No matter where we are or what we do in life, whether it is fame and fortune, friends, love, money, family, relatives, and all other human relationships, we need to know when and how to progress or retreat as appropriate.

When a machine is working well, it runs and stops accordingly. If we are to have well-rounded relationships and reasoning, we should be able to progress and retreat just as well. Wise readers, can you do that accordingly?

MAGNETIC FIELDS AND ENERGY

Every person in the world, regardless of his/her social status or wealth, has energy. In the universe, each of the planets in the solar system and the mountains and rivers on earth all have their energy source. In daily life, we make use of solar energy, hydroelectric energy, fire, and the most controversial energy source in the world today, nuclear energy.

There is energy in everything on earth, whether it is a tree, a flower, or even a drop of water. Even garbage can be recycled to produce energy or fertilizer, providing helpful conditions for people. So everything and every person in the world provides energy for each other.

Buddhism teaches that all sentient beings have Buddha Nature. Buddha Nature is energy. Therefore, since people have the capacity to become Buddha, there is energy involved in the process of committing one's life to the Dharma. However, many people have forgotten about their innate energy and pursue other external energy sources.

Nowadays, a lot of people like to create mysteries out of nothing. They have created the term "magnetic field." They not only tell people that some places have a strong magnetic field but also claim that even a piece of rock, wood, or ore has its own magnetic field. Many people advertise such gimmicks to make a profit. They vividly describe a certain person, a particular tree, a kind of pearl, or someone's hands or eyes as having magnetic fields. In reality, we get fire when we drill wood, sparks fly when we knock two pieces of rock together, and even our clothes get static. These are all natural energy sources within our universe. However, when people use the term "magnetic field" to describe a phenomenon, they cloak it in a shroud of mystery and encourage those who are already curious about it.

Actually, the largest energy source or magnetic field is in our minds. Many people are sad and weak because they do not believe in their own Buddha Nature and the energy source of all phenomena, but they dramatically describe where, who and what objects have magnetic fields, so that those who are interested in mystic

things will pursue them. Such delusion!

Artists can paint beautiful portraits, cooks can prepare gourmet dishes, and magicians can work their magic. They each have their own wonder and techniques, and their skills are also different magnetic fields. We should realize that there is nothing curious about magnetic fields, as they are easily available in everyday life. So why do people have to use the term "magnetic field" to create mysteries in the world?

Hopefully, those who are overly consumed with the idea of "magnetic fields" and other mysteries in the universe can view them with a rational mind, and not be deluded anymore!

LETTING GO AND PICKING UP

We should conduct ourselves as if we were a suitcase. We should be able to pick things up and let things go. If we only pick things up, life becomes difficult and burdensome. If we only let things go, life might become inconvenient if we need these things later. Therefore, we should pick up and let go as appropriate.

People often remind us "let go, let go!" If we cannot let go of fame and fortune, we will be tied down by them. If we do not let go of the joy of being together and the sorrow of departing, we will struggle and suffer endlessly. When we cannot let go of money, social status and love, we will forever be tangled in their mesh. If we do not let go of gossip, gains and losses, and good and evil, we will never gain peace.

It is good to be able to let go, but it is more difficult to pick up. If someone has let go of everything in life, what is left? Therefore, it is important to pick up right views, right actions, right speech, right thoughts, compassion, morals, good connections, and diligence. Without these, where does the meaning and value of life lie?

Buddhism teaches people to let go; however, after letting go of something or someone, we should be able to pick up something or someone else. In taking up, we should also be able to let go. The hardest things in life to let go of are family, spouse, children, love, and wealth. We always carry the load and suffer for them. So it is reasonable for Buddhism to advise us to let go sometimes.

People who care for their country and fellow citizens may not be able to let go of them. Similarly, people who are concerned about social harmony also will not be able to let go. People filled with righteousness cannot let go of violations of social justice and may become cynical and resentful. However, if they let go of everything, they will no longer be the heroes and sages who carry the torch for the social causes that benefit humanity. Thus, there must be a value system for letting go and picking up. We let go and pick up only after careful consideration and weighing of priorities. Letting go and picking up are two sides of the same coin and are equally important.

Ksitigarbha Bodhisattva let go of worldly fame and fortune and took up teaching the Dharma to the beings in hell in the effort to liberate them. Avalokitesvera Bodhisattva let go of his position to attain Buddhahood in the Western Pure Land and took up the challenge of relieving the suffering of sentient beings in the Saha world. In the Buddhist sutras, much has been written in praise of practitioners who let go and even more about those who take up the bodhisattva path.

Anger, jealousy, sorrow and suffering are too heavy to carry in the human heart. We should let them go. However, responsibility, social justice, and compassionate vows should be taken up. Therefore, we need to remind ourselves that we should be like a suitcase. When we need to pick up, we do so, and when we should let go, we let go.

FANTASIES AND IDEALS

When we were young, we all dreamed of being Tarzan, Peter Pan, a scientist, a literary scholar, or an inventor. But dreams can turn out to be either a fantasy or an ideal.

What is a fantasy? It is the impossible, the unreal, the confused and the superficial. According to the *Diamond Sutra*, "it is like a bubble or a dream, a drop of dew or a bolt of lightning." In the world of illusions, a fantasy is a thought that is both impractical and impossible to realize.

What is an ideal? To have an ideal is to have a goal, a plan, and a process for its realization. An ideal has potential and possibilities. However, there are some people who would rather live in a world of fantasies. Because of their unwillingness to leave their fantasies behind, they are governed by whims and are unrealistic in their pursuits. Trapped by their own imaginations, they live disappointed and lonely lives that are hollow and unreal. Worse yet, they can become paranoid and blame everyone and everything but themselves. All these troubles are brought on by fantasy.

We will not reap the benefits of meditation if we lack concentration and are surrounded by illusions. By being mindful of the Buddha, we can focus our minds and combat delusions. However, one thought of the Buddha is not the ultimate cure. We need to further harness distractions with right thought, which in turn needs to be countered with non-thought. "A thought is non-thought and a non-thought is a thought." That is the cultivation we need to be mindful of the Buddha.

Fanciful thinking will not get us anywhere in our business affairs. Is it possible to become the president of the United States on the strength of a fantasy? Is it possible to be the next Bill Gates because we dream about it everyday? A fantasy is just an illusion; it is not tangible. What we need instead is for real causes and conditions to come together.

The *Lotus Sutra* tells us not to be afraid of fantasy arising but to be fearful of belated awakening. Illusions are not serious when we are aware of them. Being awakened is to put our ideals into practice and to translate them into realities.

Although most people wish for immortality, the fountain of youth is nothing but a fantasy. Although some Taoist practitioners desire a rapid path to enlightenment, how many of them really succeed? If we choose to go against current trends, we will experience nothing but failure. It is just not possible to realize a dream of utopia amidst internal strife and chaos.

Scientists are full of theories waiting to be put into practice; some capable politicians are filled with aspirations waiting to be realized. For them to have any kind of success in turning their dreams into realities and achieving their goals, they need to have the necessary strength and resources. Armed with determination and ingenuity, scientists were able to invent airplanes and automobiles, and to discover electricity. It is with power and strong resolve that politicians have hoped for freedom, democracy, peace and order. People like George Washington of the United States, Dr. Sun Yat Sen of China, Mahatma Gandhi of India, and Nelson Mandela of South Africa had the strength to realize their ideals, and in doing so made a difference in the world.

For more than 2,000 years, Buddhism has been a religion for people, and has propagated great ideals in the teachings of "Humanistic Buddhism." Its goal is to create a Pure Land on earth for the family, society and the mind by disseminating the seeds of compassion and sending forth the fragrance of happiness. It was not too long ago when the first seeds of Humanistic Buddhism were planted, and now it has blossomed into a tree that bears infinite fruits. Therefore, any ideal can be translated into reality, as long as it meets the needs of the people.

TRUTH AND LIES

Once upon a time, "Truth" and "Lies" went bathing in the river. Lies got out of the water first and secretly put on the clothes of Truth. As Truth pled with Lies to return his clothes, Lies refused, no matter what Truth said. Truth had principles and ideals and refused to put on Lies' clothes. So he went home without a thread on his back. Since then, people see Lies wearing the clothes of Truth and respect Lies, while the naked Truth is belittled. This is how the world has confused truth and lies.

Throughout history, there have been numerous cases where minions in the imperial court cheated by using lies, but loyal ministers always used the truth to serve their country and emperors. However, human nature prefers listening to nice things. So even the famed Qing Emperor, Qianlong, who was known for his wisdom, still favored a court jester over a loyal minister.

The popular story about the "Emperor's New Clothes" is a good illustration of the power of lies. The emperor indulged in his vanity, believing the lies of his ministers, and paraded in front of his subjects naked, falsely believing that he was wearing the most supreme garment in the world. He was completely deluded. Furthermore, the deceptive and unified actions of his ministers indicated the strength of their power.

Lies are poison, coated with sugar. The story about the boy who cried wolf is proof of their harm. On the other hand, the story of George Washington chopping down the cherry tree is a powerful demonstration of how important it is to be honest.

Lies can become the truth when they are repeated. However, while Lies was able to pull the wool over people's eyes at the time, clothes wear out, so reality will eventually be discovered. People may not accept Truth immediately, but as time goes by its innate character will be appreciated.

In the end, truth is truth, and a lie is a lie. Lies may fool people sometimes but not always. Similarly, the truth may lose its appeal for the time being, but not for a lifetime. As Christians say, "Angels return to angels and Satan belongs to Satan." Buddhism also teaches, "Those in the Buddha realm remain there, and those with the evil stay where they are." After all, white is white, black is black. There are so many in the world who confuse the truth with lies. They can succeed for a moment but cannot fool people for long. So it would be wise to use caution in our dealings with different people and situations.

THE ROOSTER AND THE DUCK

Someone once compared the character of the Chinese people to a rooster and that of the Japanese to a duck. When a flock of roosters gathers, as soon as one stretches out its neck and crows, the others rush forward and peck it down so that it can no longer strut about. Likewise, Chinese people find it difficult to stand out in the crowd because others are envious. The Japanese, on the other hand, are like ducks. When there is a duck up front quacking, the others immediately follow in a row. This shows that the Japanese have team spirit and can follow their leader.

Looking around the world, we can observe the character of people in other nations. For instance, Americans have the character of an eagle. They proclaim themselves to be the big brother of the world and are always ready to fight a battle in the name of defending freedom. Indians have the character of a dog, loyal and honest. Jewish people have the character of a monkey, intelligent and quick. Mongolians have the character of a camel, tolerant and responsible. Tibetans have the character of an ox, hardworking and suffering. Germans have the character of a horse, open and fast. The French have the character of a deer, romantic and fanciful. The British have the character of an elephant, gentlemanly and steady. Russians have the character of a polar bear, heavy but agile. Other countries have the character of swans, peacocks, lions, wolves, tigers, and leopards.

The citizens of each country resemble those of one animal or another, and others can easily detect these differences. Naturally, all nations have strengths and shortcomings. Therefore, nations that consider themselves to be superior must improve their character so that selfishness, viciousness and craftiness are transformed into compassion, integrity, tolerance, and respect. People need to change their character and nations must as well, in order for the world to progress and to be more peaceful.

Human beings are considered supreme among all living things. They rule the world because humanity enjoys culture and thinking, unlike animals, for whom food is the only mission in life. Human beings have indeed contributed much to the world.

Organizations that advocate peace and human rights, such as the Red Cross and Amnesty International, have made major contributions to humanity.

Today the world is increasingly more serious about protecting the environment and endangered species, and maintaining beautiful landscapes and cultural heritage sites. So human beings are not entirely like dogs, cats, roosters, ducks, cows, horses, lions or tigers. How can humans progress in the future? This is not just a test of people's wisdom but also an indicator of whether they are peace loving or belligerent.

CHANGING AND UNCHANGING

Everything in the universe is always changing. We can say that what does not change in the world is change itself. Nature can be changeable and unchangeable. Things will either change or remain the same.

The "*Sutra of the Forty-two Sections*" says, "The world is impermanent, and the country is fragile." A Song Dynasty scholar once said, "My life is only momentary" and "If we do not change our principles when viewing all phenomena, all things and self will have no end." Tang Dynasty poet Li Bai once wrote, Do you not see your parents in front of bright mirror bemoaning their gray hair-in the morning like black silk, at evening turned to snow?

We may not detect any changes in the mountains, but they are always changing in endless ways. The sun rises and sets everyday, seemingly unchanged, but the reality is that the earth revolves to a different position every day. While the change of the four seasons happens the same way each year, in reality the four seasons have different temperatures and scenery. We eat and sleep everyday-this does not change, but energy, spirit, mood, and external conditions are constantly changing.

Change is not necessarily bad. Human relations, daily matters, and mind change all the time. Change can be from bad to good. It can mean progress and hope as we change from less to more, from poor to wealthy, or from sick to healthy. However, things can also change for the worse, for example: the downfall of a government, the breakdown of a marriage, the mutiny of troops, a change of heart, a change for the worse in health, drastic changes in the landscape, climate change, the passing of time, or the demise of a friendship.

However, we should not change our goals in life too easily, even though the way to achieve our goals is to change according to circumstances. We can only survive if we are able to change and adjust according to these circumstances. We need to change our methods of learning in order to adapt ourselves to a new society. Life that remains unchanged only leaves us stagnant.

As the social environment continues to change, our values may do the same. If we want others to change their impression of us, we need to transform ourselves. In order to compete in the market, we have to come up with new ideas to attract more business. Similarly, the management of corporations should be reassessed from time to time and renewed accordingly. We should remember, though, that people who change their minds easily often appear unreliable. Only by being honest in business and not changing prices randomly will we earn the trust of others.

Mountains, rivers, and the earth, and even our home decor, real estate values, and contracts will all change. Only justice and truth remain unchanged, as do the lessons of history. True love and a steadfast heart do not change. In fact, the truth that all phenomena endure the stages of existence, growth, decay, and extinction; the cycle of birth, sickness, aging, and death; and the cardinal truth of cause, effect, and karmic retribution, does not change. Loyalty to our country, respect for our leaders, the pursuit of truth, and our inherent pure nature should not change.

We face the world's myriad of changes with unchanging principles. But we change if a situation requires adjustment so that we can move on in life. We can only hope that all things change when needed, and remain unchanged as warranted. For all that is benevolent and beautiful, we hope they remain unchanged; otherwise, if these things change from better to worse, then it is better that they not change at all.

THE SPIRIT OF A BLADE OF GRASS

Never take a blade of grass lightly! A small blade peeks out of the top of a wall or the side of a cliff. No matter how the wind blows, or how the sun and rain beat on it, it stands proudly. It wavers gently with the wind, and quietly displays its life force. As the highest form of living beings, if humans do not value life and work hard, we stand humbled in front of the small blade of grass. The spirit of a blade of grass is in its perseverance in the face of hardships and in its not being ashamed of being small.

In our surroundings, we can easily see how a small spark can set a field on fire. Small brooks form large rivers and seas. A small seed grows into a tree, laden with fruit. A small screw affects how smoothly a machine runs. Small is not to be taken lightly! Some objects may be small; but their functions are great.

As the Buddhist saying goes, "There is a world in each flower and a Buddha in every leaf." There is a universe even in a grain of sand or a tiny pebble. A small prince grows up to inherit the throne and to rule the land. A young novice monk will learn and cultivate over time and become a king of the Dharma and a teacher of humanity. A small dragon can grow big and strong and create storms and wind, with all their magnificence and force.

In Buddhism, cultivated monks helped the lives of many with simple acts and short phrases of wisdom. They were able to convince warlords and invaders on the warpath to spare hundreds of thousands of lives. Saving a country from massacre and pillage with just a short saying makes us truly appreciate the importance of smallness.

Ksudrapanthaka, a disciple of the Buddha, was enlightened while sweeping the floor. The seven-year-old maiden, Nagakanya, was able to teach Mahayana Buddhism. Chan Patriarch Bodhidharma said, "Give me your mind and I'll settle it for you." Upon hearing this, Chan Master Huike became the patriarch of his time. Chan Master Gweishen asked, "Isn't carrying a rock around in your mind heavy?" Chan Master Wenyi was given the opportunity to gain enlightenment by being asked that question. A young novice monk at Mount Putuo established a tradi-

tional monastery. In history, many who started with a low rank or were very young became great heroes and heroines of their times. As the saying goes, "A word can break or make a nation!" Indeed, being small should not be taken lightly.

With the spirit of a small blade of grass a person can beat the odds and prevail and go anywhere, whether it is high on a mountaintop or deep into the ocean! An elegant room does not need to be large, and it does not take many fragrant flowers to spread perfume. Humans only need the spirit of a blade of grass to develop their lives in the world.

THE CENTIPEDE

The following story circulated on the Internet. "One day, all the insects gathered for a general meeting. Halfway through, they discovered they needed more soft drinks. As they were debating who should go buy them, the centipede volunteered to go. He was gone for a long time, and everyone was getting anxious. Finally, someone decided to go look for him. When they opened the door, they found the centipede still there putting shoes on his one hundred feet!"

This joke is intended to ridicule the legislative process of many governments, where numerous bills and proposals are discussed with few actual results. Just as the centipede took a long time to put on his shoes, the way legislators work is slow and disagreeable.

This story also reminds us of how people often behave at meetings. They meet and talk, but they reach no conclusions, or when there are conclusions, no actions are ever taken. There are people who learn but do not practice what they learn or do not practice; and even if they practice, they do not care about the results. They are all like the centipede putting on his shoes.

A few decades ago a tongue-in-cheek study rated the efficiency of different countries. The conclusions were as follows: Germans do, but do not talk; Japanese do as they talk; and Chinese talk, but do not do. One might say that these characteristics are due to cultural differences. This reminds us of the popular story of the turtle who raced the hare. The hare was arrogant and slacked off, giving the turtle the opportunity to overtake him. There is another story about two pilgrims, one rich, one poor. The rich man thought he could do his pilgrimage anytime, because he could take a car there. He waited year after year, without taking action. On the other hand, the poor man, who could only walk there because he could not afford transportation, completed his pilgrimage and made it home within a year.

Regarding one's cultivation, it is better for us to "walk a foot" rather than "talk a mile". The snail's speed has long been discarded by people. In modern life, speed has become so important.

Whether we fly in planes, go by train or drive in cars, we want to move fast and reach our destination as quickly as possible. Speed symbolizes efficiency and worthiness. But we should remember the proverb "less haste, more speed."

Once there was an artist who sculpted a piece of artwork in a month. Another artist took three years but still could not finish a piece. When the patron asked him why he took so long, he retorted, "Is there time to art?" Actually, even with art there should be a timeline. Without time limits, the artwork cannot be appreciated in the present lifetime. What purpose does that serve?

In today's world, we emphasize economics in life. We all need to budget according to our income and calculate the amount of expenses for the day, the month, and the year. At work, we need to plan how much we can accomplish in an hour, a day, or a month. Without efficient planning, tasks can drag on forever.

In defense of our nation, if we do not work efficiently, we will still be planning a battle strategy when rockets and missiles are flying over our heads. In starting a business, we should not be jealous of how others make more money than we do. We should appreciate how efficiently they plan. Even in our cultivation, there is a "deadline for enlightenment" which allows no delays. We should face the limited time we have in life and be efficient in what we do. We should never be like the centipede, putting on shoes and wasting so much precious time.

CITY LIGHTS

Light connotes brightness and provides a sense of security to people. Light is the opposite of darkness. The darker it is the more light is needed to illuminate things.

When city lights come on after dark, it indicates a prosperous metropolis. Colorful neon signs flash and beckon those going out for a night in the city to start their evening of revelry. But it is also the time when tired birds return to their nests and those ending a day's work seek the warmth of their homes.

On the other hand, as city lights go on, unwholesome elements and evildoers come out to roost, robbing, stealing, and scheming to harm others, as most crimes take place in the dark of the night. People's hearts tend to be a little weaker at night, and it seems a little easier to get sick. The sounds of ambulance sirens at night are particularly traumatic.

Day-workers like it best when city lights come on because it is time to go home, but the homeless fear darkness most for the loneliness it brings, since they have no home to return to. In the same way that circumstances are different for each of us, our feelings toward glittering city lights also vary. A satisfied person does not understand the pangs of a hungry one, just as those living under the shelter of brightness find it difficult to appreciate the hardships of struggling in darkness.

Most people work during the day and go home when the city lights come on. However, there are those who sleep in the daytime and start work in the evening. For instance, police walking their beats, janitors cleaning buildings, and journalists writing for newspapers. There are service workers, such as hospital staff and firemen, who also work night shifts. Even when the weather is cold and wet, the coast guard and emergency workers are still at their posts, on guard all night. Their spirit is truly admirable.

While teamwork prevails during the day, others work through the night on their own projects under a lamp. Students cram for their studies, and writers create in the quiet of the night. They make the best use of time, diligently striving for their ideals in life. So, while some people engage in unwholesome acts when city lights are lit, others are out there doing good deeds.

POLARIZATION

The two ends of our globe are called the North Pole and the South Pole. People sometimes use the word 'polarizing' to describe a person whose character is extreme. It also describes opposites such as good and bad, wealthy and poor, large and small, right and wrong. People with extreme personalities are the most difficult to get along with because they are attached to either existence or non-existence. They either speak well or badly of something. They have no middle ground and do not understand the meaning of life on the Middle Way.

The mind also traverses between "two poles" on a daily basis. We sometimes go to heaven, and other times fall into hell. It is a hard life wandering back and forth between the two poles. When faced with setbacks, we often become depressed and pessimistic. When things are going smoothly, we are invigorated and become active and optimistic. In reality, if we are too extreme in our pursuits in life, happiness may result in sorrow. On the other hand, if we are too pessimistic, we can be so depressed that we may even want to kill ourselves.

However, life is not really that hopeless. As the saying goes, "Heaven will always leave a door open." As long as we can think further, change direction, take a different position, get into another frame of mind, and look at things from another angle, anything can turn around. The opportunity to turn over a new leaf is always there for us.

Polarization in life or in our way of thinking is difficult because it means either the freezing cold of the two Poles, or the sweltering heat of the Equator. A life of hardship is too cold and passionless, and lacks strength; while a life of pleasure is too hot, and leaves us lost. Therefore, Buddhism advocates the Middle Way of life.

In the Buddha's time, there was a musician named Sronakotivimsa. He became a monk and asked the Buddha how to cultivate himself. The Buddha asked what his profession had been, and he replied that he had been a musician.

The Buddha asked, "What happens when you play a string instrument and the strings are too tight?"

Sronakotivimsa replied, "The strings break!"

The Buddha then asked, "What if the strings are too loose?"

He answered, "They won't make any sound!"

The Buddha explained, "Cultivation is the same. If we become too tight, we will be stressed. When we are too loose, we will be listless and lazy. In seeking the appropriate and middle way, music will flow easily."

People today tend to go to extremes. They want to be the most attractive, eat the best foods, wear the latest fashion, and be friends with the best. Anything less than "the best" cannot be accepted. People who are extreme fail to appreciate the meaning of the Middle Way, and life loses its objectivity for them.

The Buddha practiced asceticism in the snowy mountains for six years. Living an inhuman life, he ate only sesame grains as food and meditated until birds built nests on his head. He finally realized that the practice of such extreme suffering only increased troubles and wore out the body and mind. Thus, he gave up asceticism and crossed the Nilajan River. After receiving an offering of goat's milk from a shepherd girl, he recovered his strength. As he sat under the bodhi tree, he contemplated, "This mind should not be attached to either existence or non-existence." As he eradicated the two extremes, he attained perfect enlightenment, gazing at the stars on the evening of the eighth day of the twelfth lunar month, at the age of 31.

Therefore, if you have an extreme personality, do change it and take the Middle Way!

MIGRATORY BIRDS

Migratory birds breed in cold regions and fly to warmer areas when winter comes. Tropical birds fly to cooler regions to stay cool when the hot summer approaches.

We often witness these migratory birds moving from one region to another every year. However, we should not think that they are so free. In reality, there are many hardships. They may die in the mountains and oceans en route, and their deaths and injuries cause hardships to their families. When they reach their destination, people or animals may hunt them. For example, in the Hengchuan Mountain region in Taiwan many shrikes are killed every year for food.

In order to train their offspring for survival, migratory birds suffer many deaths and injuries. But they still accept the risks and never cease in their mission.

People are like migratory birds. They leave home early and return late in the evening, often traveling out of town to different regions. At the end of the year, they always want to come home to visit their families. Like today's immigrants, they move from one region that has grown uncomfortable for them to live in another place. They travel far and wide, crossing oceans and continents. While every region in the world has immigrants, eventually they want to return to their homeland to seek out their roots.
Migratory birds do not forget their living habits and the education of their offspring. They have no fear of sacrifice, and strive without ceasing. However, many Chinese immigrants these days have moved to other countries and become overwhelmed by the current times. As they assimilate, they lose their basic foundation and identity and become so-called "bananas," yellow on the outside and white on the inside. This is a shame.

Among migratory birds, some may be eliminated by their own kind. For instance, when a mother swallow nesting on the beam of a house discovers a baby bird that is not strong enough, she would rather push it out of the nest to fall to its death, because she does not want her species to wane. We sometimes see Canadian wild geese that have lived an easy existence and put on

too much weight. They have trouble flying because they are too heavy and cannot migrate to warmer regions. They freeze to death in the winter. Once swans are fed and cared for by humans, they become complacent and do not know that they should move on.

Salmon in North America swim upstream each year. Even when they are hurt badly, they still want to spawn where they were born. There is a kind of butterfly in the United States, the monarch, which originates in Mexico. After a flying relay involving five generations, it finds its way back home.

Animals are brave enough to challenge nature in the struggle to breed and pursue their roots. Why can't humans be like migratory birds?

THE LANGUAGE OF FLOWERS

There is no doubt that people can talk, but what about animals, birds and fish? While we do not understand the meaning of the sounds they make, we often hear horses bray and cows moo when they feel like it. Birds in the forest call and chirp to one another from one tree to the next. How can we say that they don't have their own language?

What about flowers, grass and trees? Do they have a language, too? In nature, some languages are verbal while others are silent. In Buddhism, it is said that "The noise of a brook is a broad long tongue," meaning the language of sound, while "The colors of the mountains are a pure body," referring to the language of silence.

Some people can be very articulate and express themselves well, while others cannot. Some people have lived for decades and cannot even handle their own language, not to mention learn another one. On the other hand, others are fluent in half a dozen or even ten languages. Sometimes, we praise a person as being very understanding of others' wishes. In Chinese, we call women who can do so "understanding flowers."

As for the language of flowers, carnations express the care of motherly love, white lilies purity, lilacs first love, magnolias trust, and morning glories the love between a man and a woman. In the West, roses not morning glories represent love.

In reality, Chinese plants have spoken to the world for a long time. There are spring orchids, summer water lilies, autumn chrysanthemums, and winter plum blossoms. Orchids in the spring tell us they are hermits in the mountains. Water lilies in the summer speak about their patience and purity. "When it gets so hot that people sweat, even the centers of the flowers in the lily pond are fragrant." Autumn chrysanthemums are straight and steady: "Withered chrysanthemums still have stems to brave the frost." They can withstand the cold and hold their own with dignity. Winter plum blossoms have no fear of ice and snow. They outshine others, standing proud in bloom. "Without bone-chilling cold, how can the fragrance of plum blossoms be profuse?"

Flowers have their individual characteristics. Therefore,

countries around the world usually select their national flower as a symbol of their spirit. China uses the peony, a sign of nobility and prosperity, and Taiwan's plum blossom is symbolic of perseverance and eminence. There are other well-known national flowers, such as Japan's cherry blossom, Holland's tulip, India's water lily, Nepal's azalea, Russia's sunflower, and the American and British rose.

The many flowers tell the world their origins, spirit, essence, and value. They speak the Dharma, especially with their blooming and withering: the world's changes, suffering, emptiness, and impermanence. However, even though everything is impermanent, flowers still hope to bloom again. There is the following verse: "A year ago today, by this door, people's faces and the peach blossoms were rosy red. Now the faces are nowhere to be found, but the peach blossoms are still smiling in the spring breeze."

Not only do flowers speak the Dharma, but everyday nature also shows us the changes of the world. However, "while falling flowers have a purpose, the flowing river does not care." Wise readers, can you see clearly the meaning of falling flowers? Can you understand the truth taught by the sound of flowing water? Can you be like peach blossoms and think about the spring, summer, autumn, and winter of your future lives?

THE POISONOUS SNAKE METAPHOR

There are many things that are difficult to understand in this world, so we need metaphors to help us understand them. The following is a discussion of metaphors about poisonous snakes.

Since ancient times, the poisonous snake has been used as a symbol of evil and deviance. When beautiful women delude people, they are often described as venomous snakes. While some people are willing to die for money, they cannot stand seeing others get rich, so they say, "Gold is a poisonous snake." We also sometimes describe a person's heart as being "as poisonous as a serpent" or "as greedy as a snake swallowing an elephant."

In reality, poisonous snakes have no intention of harming people. They only strike because they feel they are under attack by humans. As long as they are left undisturbed, they will not attack people without a reason. Likewise, money itself is neither good nor bad. Gold can actually be used to save someone in difficulty. However, when people are greedy, money will become a poisonous snake and kill them.

In other words, gold and money are not poisonous snakes to a benevolent and righteous person. Similarly, a poisonous snake is just a typical reptile to a kind person, because it causes no harm to anyone. In this world, good or bad, poisonous or otherwise are just the results of how we treat one another. Humans say lions and tigers are vicious because they eat people and therefore should be killed. However, from the standpoint of lions and tigers, humans transgress their living space, so people should be eradicated instead.

Life is actually equal. When we fail to respect and love others, they will treat us with similar ill intentions. A snake's venom is only for self-defense and not for harming others. Human beings and snakes are two species of animals. However, people refuse to give any of their living space to snakes to survive. Instead, they catch them and use them for specialty dishes or medicine. In protecting their lives, poisonous snakes have to use venom as their defense. It is like beautiful women. Their beauty is not meant to delude others, but people become deluded themselves. If it is not

the intention of men to seduce women or take advantage of them, then even if women are as poisonous as snakes and scorpions, what can they possibly do?

Gold is not a poisonous snake. Actually, we can benefit society with gold. We can build roads and bridges and do many good deeds for the world. However, if we use the same gold to traffic drugs, smuggle, take advantage of others or engage in unlawful activities, we cannot blame it on gold when our bad deeds catch up to us.

Poisonous snakes are not to be feared, because the selfishness in our hearts is actually far more fearsome!

A SINGLE SPARK

The *Ekottara-Agama* says, "A prince may be little but he can grow up to govern. A small fire may not be roaring, but a spark can ignite a plain. A dragon may appear small but can bring rain when the time is right, and a novice monk may be young, but he can become a king of the Dharma to liberate people." This illustrates that we should not underestimate or look down upon the strength of the small.

There is a Taiwanese saying, "Young men steal carrots; big men steal cows." This means children may start stealing small things and enjoy the taste, and desire more and more. So they steal larger and larger things. Then it is too late to change.

How do we prevent an epidemic of unwholesome deeds? We must be cautious at the start and cover all angles. If we do not begin with the right views and benevolent behaviors, and fail to turn ourselves around for the better in time, we will eventually end up with unwholesome habits that are irrevocable. When we step on frost and snow, we should realize that the weather will get colder from then on, and thick ice will form eventually. The *Dharmapada* says, "Do not belittle small bad deeds and think there is no harm. Water drops may be little, but they accumulate to fill a large container. All wrongdoings that become major start out small."

Ants burrowing small crevices in the earth can cause a large dam to collapse. A small cigarette butt can cause a huge forest fire. A minor cold can turn into pneumonia, and a tiny snowball can roll into an avalanche. So if we do not stop things when they are small, irreparable damage can be done. However, people today are self-centered and often do what pleases them. Their reckless damage to nature over time has resulted in avalanches, floods, and landslides, harming both the good earth and human beings.

"One bad apple spoils the whole bunch." Therefore, a small personal misbehavior can cause a person, a society, a country or even the world immense loss and regret. If every person can start doing good deeds by saying a word of praise, smiling at others,

having positive thoughts, giving someone a helping hand, and being mindful of protecting the environment, conditions will change and the world can be improved.

We often see a statue in parks, government buildings, and art museums of a little boy urinating. This Belgian boy doused a fire with his pee in the nick of time, saving the lives of tens of thousands of people. A small act can, therefore, benefit the world and save many lives.

The ancients said, "What is big starts from humble and small beginnings and grows. Small drops of water can form large deep gorges. Tiny specks of dust can pile up into mountains. Half paces can eventually turn into a thousand miles, and small acts of benevolence can accumulate into great merit." These all teach us to be aware of the potentiality of what is small.

THE DAZZLING WORLD

Have you seen a dazzling world?

When flowers bloom in the park in their myriad colors and wildlife prowls in the woods, or when city lights are lit and men and women wearing their finest go out for an evening of dancing and drinking-these are dazzling worlds of color and glitz. Society is resplendent with color, human sentiments, and strange phenomena. There are a variety of theories and unconventional studies in the academic world. We live in a world full of volatility and stability, positivity and negativity.

A glitzy world can be bewitching, as it is full of glamour and glory. It is filled with temptations, and people caught off guard may be overwhelmed by its color and vibrancy and not want to leave if they lose their sense of direction.

In reality, besides the dazzling, external world, there are other worlds for different people: the ancients, modern people, men, women, Eastern and Western people. Even the Buddhas and bodhisattvas have their own worlds, for instance: the Medicine Buddha's World of Pure Crystal, Amitabha Buddha's World of Ultimate Bliss, and Avalokitesvera Bodhisattva's World of Compassion. Each region and ethnicity has its own dazzling world as well. Writers, scientists, entertainment artists, painters, the wealthy and even the homeless and nomads all have individual, internal worlds.

The *Analects of Confucius* says, "The wise are in accord, without the need to form parties; the mean form parties, but are in discord." Every person wants to create a dazzling world for himself or herself that is different from that of others. What should it be like? An individual's dazzling world should show off one's special talents, full of fragrance that can be shared with others; joyful for the individual and yet able to be mutually owned with another; filled with purity that can be one with nature and strong in benevolence, justice, and ethics. It should be a world of truth, kindness, and beauty. If we concentrate diligently on our individual worlds, we will not be deluded by the dazzling, external world.

Though the dazzling, external world can be blinding, many

people are so attached to it that they dream of gaining immortality. On the other hand, we should not resent our presence here so much that we want to end our life. As we live in this dazzling world of ours, we can walk through the bushes of a hundred flowers with not a leaf attached to us. In Buddhism, it is also said that we establish places of cultivation, transient like the moon's shadow over water, for performing Dharma functions that are illusive like empty flowers. This means that all things are impermanent and we need not be attached to glory or glitz. We can be like the lotus flower described by a Chinese poet, "Born out of mud and not tainted, bathed by the green ripples and not seductive."

While the dazzling, external world is false and misleading, our internal world should be windless and calm, without blossom or fragrance. While the external world is full of people fighting for status and profit, in pursuit of fame, money and pleasures, the internal world should be content and at ease.

SHOOTING STARS

Shooting stars are beautiful, and yet they are only momentary. However, people always pause to praise their brightness. Life should be like a shooting star, creating a moment of eternity in our brief lives.

In the past, the Chinese always perceived shooting stars to be inauspicious. They were even interpreted as an omen that a great man would pass away or that a disaster was coming. Western people, however, feel that shooting stars bring good luck and make a wish when they see them, believing that their wishes will come true. Now, every June and July many Chinese people crowd into mountain areas, marveling at the brilliance of shooting stars as they cross the sky. They imitate Western people and make a quick wish, hoping their wishes will be fulfilled forever.

In reality, it is not important whether you have longevity or not; what is important is to live with meaning and values. People praise thousand-year-old pines and cypresses for their longevity. However, they also praise shooting stars for their brief appearance and disappearance. Just like an epiphyllum, which blooms and emits an amazing fragrance on just one quiet night and like lightning bugs that dance delightfully illuminating the darkness of the night for only fourteen nights, a rainbow also displays its instantaneous yet brilliant colors after the rain. Whether it is forever or only for a moment, it is always good to be beautiful.

Human beings are the same. Some never left any memorable footsteps for others to remember them by during their lives; others are remembered for their radiance, even though they lived like a shooting star, only for a brief time.

Power, status, and fortune are only momentary in life. Youthfulness is not permanent either, and we cannot bring money and property with us when we go. We should all be concerned about how we can leave the light of life behind for others to always remember. Sima Qian, a famed historian of the Han Dynasty, once said, "People all die. Death can be as heavy as Mount Tai, or as light as a goose feather. It all depends on how differently we apply life." We should be able to light up our lives

and give warmth to others through service and caring. We need to bring into full play our skills and knowledge so as to contribute to society, benefiting humanity in order to earn its respect and to live in its memory.

Throughout the history of the world, some well-known religious people, political leaders, great generals, poets and musicians achieved amazing and admirable accomplishments in their brief lives. Therefore people's accomplishments are not dependent on the length of their lives, the level of their status, or the amount of their money. They hinge on the depth of their morality and contribution to humanity.

In reality, there are also shooting stars during the daytime, but they go unnoticed. At night, the falling stars appear brighter and more attractive because of the darkness and catch people's attention. Therefore, we should not fear darkness or setbacks in life. As long as we work hard, we will certainly shine in the dark.

People compare life to a dream, an illusion, the morning dew, or a play. But when our accomplishments and merits benefit fellow human beings and our nation, it does not matter whether our lives are as brief as a bubble or as momentary as a shooting star.

FLOWING WATER
STAGNANT WATER

We can easily tell the difference between water in a stagnant pool and water in a small flowing brook. Without any flow, stagnant water is lifeless. There is no activity and no future. The brook, on the other hand, may be small, but it runs forth and overcomes obstacles. There is an endless future in its flow.

Life is like running water. It flows without end. Our thoughts arise without ceasing, flowing like water. The Yogacara School of Buddhism compares the eighth consciousness, Alaya-vijnana, to a waterfall.

Life is indeed like water! However, some people are conservative and stubborn. Their lives and minds are like a cesspool because they refuse to interact with other sentient beings. They are of no benefit to others. They study hard, but knowledge becomes dead in their minds because they do not use it well. Their lives are stagnant pools. Others find it hard to cope with life, and they cannot get along with others. If they do not discover their talents, skills, or potential, the water of life will not flow for them, and they are as good as dead.

The water of life stagnates when we find life inadequate, are unwilling to benefit others, or refuse to share what we have. A poet once wrote, "Why is the canal's water so clean and clear? Because it is supplied from a fountainhead of flowing water." When we have prajna-wisdom, we have running water in our lives. We should make good use of life's flowing water.

We moisten withering crops with the flowing water of timely rain.
We douse the flames of anger with the flowing water of tolerance.
We cleanse the defilements of the body and mind with the flowing water of wisdom.
We quench the thirsts of life with the flowing water of the Dharma.

Not only is life like water; but other matters are similar to it

as well. A relationship is like water. If you only keep it in reserve, then it stagnates; when we interact and connect with others, it comes alive. Money is like water. If we do not use it, then it is stagnant water. When we use money wisely, then it is flowing water. As water follows its course, we should follow ours. We should have the fighting spirit to go against all odds, so that life becomes active and running, like flowing water. The mind is also like water. Our minds should move like running water. When the mind is active, water flows.

When a cup is broken, the cup itself cannot be recovered, and the water in it falls to the earth. When the temperature is high, water evaporates and then condenses into rain and again comes back to life as water. Therefore, life is like water that flows in all directions. Whether we can find the true value of life depends on whether our lives are like stagnant or flowing water.

THE HELMSMAN

A boat traveling on the ocean needs a helmsman to steer it home safely; a plane flying in the sky requires a pilot to ensure a safe landing. Explorers and travelers rely on compasses and other equipment to determine the right direction in order to arrive at their destinations safely.

The world is also like an ocean. It often feels like we are in the middle of nowhere. We need the ability to steer the helm correctly so that we will not lose our way. Some people rely on knowledge to navigate through life; others rely on experience to take hold of their future; some rely on good causes and conditions to help them move toward the correct goals in life; and others rely on confidence and perseverance to realize their ideals. When we are young, we may be interested in learning literature, martial arts, technology, or business. We need to rely on ourselves to take the helm and determine in which direction to go. People from all walks of life can achieve the results they desire and reach their goals if they take control of the helm of their future.

From youth, some people aspire to travel in the ocean of knowledge, but they never get anywhere with their studies because they fail to assess their own abilities correctly. There are people who seek a good-looking partner in marriage, but they are not successful and become lost on the road of relationships, swept off by the wild winds of romance.

Other people vow to work for the benefit of country and society, but become distracted by fame, fortune, gains, and losses. They wander onto the wrong path instead. While some people become heads of households and guide their family members forward, there are helmsmen who steer a community, a race, or a country toward the future. Regardless of what their responsibilities may be, people at the helm must use intelligence and wisdom to set the right course for the morale of all members, so they will not lose their direction.

Some people do not know how to steer, so they follow the leadership of the wise and are able to build successful careers. Some people cannot find a helmsman in which to entrust their

faith, but they still find their path in life. However, others cannot steer themselves, are hesitant and suspicious, and do not trust the ability of others to steer them. So, even when there is direction, they lack the strength to move. They fail in the end, and are left complaining about their ill fortune.

Therefore, if we want to steer our lives correctly, we need to understand time and space well, be supported with positive causes and conditions, and have the ability to adapt to changes on the path of life. When we have the support of all of these, then we need not fear charging ahead toward the future!

The Ocean

Here are three interesting questions to consider: (1) What proportion of the Earth is covered by water and what proportion by land? (2) Which contains more treasure, the ocean or the land? (3) Is the depth of the Earth's oceans greater or lesser than the height of its mountains?

During the Tang Dynasty, a poet stated, "Three parts mountain, six parts water, one part fields." Since most of the Earth is covered by water, there are more natural resources to be found therein. And, although the peaks of our mountains rise high above the skyline, their heights are not as unfathomable as the depths of the world's oceans.

How does the ocean contribute to humankind? What inspiration does the ocean offer us? The ocean not only contains a wealth of biodiversity-rich in species and renewable resources-but also influences the global climate system, providing rain and influencing weather patterns. It is also very important economically, as it is vital to a country's rate of growth and development. For example, countries near the ocean develop much faster than inland countries; without the benefits provided by the ocean, inland countries tend to lag behind.

From afar the ocean may seem calm, but it is actually full of roaring waves and surging billows. Even professional navigators who have decades of experience do not necessarily understand its rage and mystery, for the ocean's secrets are safely hidden in its depths, away from the probing eyes of oceanographers. Although sonar and other sophisticated equipment have given us a glimpse of how profound and mysterious the ocean is, a full understanding of the ocean is still beyond our reach.

Since the ocean is the source of nourishment for life on Earth, it has come to symbolize many different things in western literature. It is known to be a storehouse of energy, but unpredictable in nature. It is not only vast but also dangerous and ruthless, for it can swallow everything in sight. From the ocean's ability to either support or capsize a vessel, we should be mindful of the fact that there are always two sides to everything, and we should adapt accordingly.

Buddhism often uses the ocean's vastness as a metaphor for the Dharma, since the teachings of the Buddha are limitless and without boundaries. "The ocean of the Dharma can only be entered through faith, and crossed through wisdom." "The mind is as boundless as the ocean and can be cultivated along with the body, if the seeds of the pure lotus are planted everywhere."

"When we penetrate the Buddhist sutras deeply, we will find wisdom as profound as the ocean." There are oceans of wisdom and compassion as well as Dharma-treasure and the path to enlightenment.

Although the boundless ocean has the incomparable ability to hold everything within, it is a place of fierce competition and unmatched cruelty, where the big devour the small and the small eat the miniscule. It is a world where countless lives are sacrificed in the name of nourishment and survival.

"While the benevolent enjoy the mountains, the wise appreciate the water." Each has its own merit. How else could we reach the mountaintop or surf the ocean's waves if they were without breadth and depth? There is simply no way for us to adequately describe and comprehend the ocean's beauty, mystery, subtlety, and diversity.

"As the mountain stood indomitable, the ocean remained unfathomable." It is the dream of every adventurer to scale the highest peak and plumb the deepest sea. The human spirit is, in fact, very much like a high mountain that is unconquerable, and the human mind is a boundless ocean that is deep and inexhaustible. Therefore, if we wish to conquer the highest mountain, we must first overcome our own spirit. If we want to reach the deepest ocean, we must first know our mind.

If our lives are as boundless and open as the ocean and sky, we will truly be free, without restraint. If we live without discriminating, like the ocean melting into the sky, we will treat every living being as a part of ourselves. Therefore, if we want to be as magnanimous as the ocean, we must first learn to broaden our minds and rid ourselves of pettiness. Only when we are as carefree as the ocean will we be able to come to the realization that life is, indeed, boundless in its infinity.

AS DEEP AS THE OCEAN

The ocean is a mysterious world. People do not fully understand its depths, treasures, and functions. Because of this, people use the ocean as a metaphor for many things in life. When life gets tough, people say, "The ocean of suffering seems limitless." When they cannot find a missing person, they feel the person is lost in the "ocean of humanity" and do not know where to look. Scholars say, "Life has a limit, but the ocean of studies does not," meaning learning should not end. When there are conflicts between people, their animosity can turn into an ocean of blood and vengeance.

The vast limitless ocean is a symbol that lasts and perseveres, representing endless hope. Lovers sometimes vow that their love for one another will "last till the ocean dries and the rocks rot." When mediating a fight, we tell the dueling parties to "move a step back and appreciate the vast ocean and sky." "City in the ocean" and "buildings in the sky" refer to mirages. "Fishing the moon from the ocean bottom" suggests a deception that gives others false hope. When "ocean waves reach the sky," the ocean has become relentless and very dangerous. "Fishing for a needle in the ocean" means the matter is extremely difficult. Going to "the ocean's corner and sky's edge" signifies separation. Because the ocean is vast and deep and yet closely connected to people, there are frequent accidents at sea.

The world is very big. However, there are always people who want to control rights over the air or water. The ocean, however, is open to all, so there are laws to oversee international waters and a court of law to handle maritime disputes.

There are many ocean metaphors. Buddhist sutras often use the ocean in metaphors as well. For instance, "The mind is limitless like the ocean, and we plant pure lotuses extensively to help sentient beings." Because the ocean of the Dharma is deep and wide, we can look for treasures within. The Buddhist saying, "When a hundred rivers flow into the ocean, they become the same salty taste," means that no matter how dirty rivers and streams may be, they cannot pollute the great ocean's purity.

Therefore, a person's character should not only be as lofty as high

mountains but also as deep and wide as the ocean.

Because the ocean of the Dharma is vast and deep, people learning the Way all wish to go deeply into the Tripitaka to acquire an ocean of wisdom. Buddhism calls the three divisions of the Buddhist Canon the "pitaka ocean" and people's minds the "mind ocean." Calling the mind an ocean encourages people to develop a mind as open and vast as the ocean.

Some people have very narrow minds. They cannot grasp the world, country, or relationships with others. Worse still, should close family members take advantage of them, they can become hostile and merciless. They are like matchboxes, with their limited capacity or toothpaste tubes that will burst if filled with just a few ounces more than they are supposed to hold. For people who have narrow minds, the vast Dharma is unable to enter and even friends and loved ones will find it difficult to gain a place, because they do not have the capacity of an ocean.

While some people have a mind as big as the ocean, others have one as narrow as a back alley. The larger the capacity of our minds, the more we can hold. The more we can hold, the greater our career will be. Therefore, if we cannot have a capacity as vast as the ocean to absorb the Dharma, our minds cannot embrace all phenomena and will not be able to benefit from the Dharma.

DEEP OR SHALLOW?

Oceans and rivers have different depths. Likewise, people's education and speech have different depths. Most people think little of those who are shallow in knowledge, and even though some people's learning is broad and deep, they may be too profound and keep others away.

When people are too profound, it is hard to resonate with others. But if they are too shallow, people look down on them. Thus, it is best to explain deep concepts with clear and understandable language. The Buddha taught the Dharma according to the characteristics of the audience and explained its meanings in ways that everyone could understand. The records of Chan Buddhism use various types of explanations, so that people can gain something from them and be enlightened.

Today, many scientists have found ways to popularize scientific knowledge for the general public. Philosophers use metaphors and stories to explain profound thinking in order to engage more people. Famous writings like "*Zhuangzi*" or Buddhist sutras like the *Lotus Sutra* and the *Maharatnakuta* display the wisdom of great teachers and philosophers who explained profound ideas using unambiguous language.

Ordinary people belittle what is only skin-deep. When acupuncturists treat patients, they insert the needles as deep or shallow as the situation requires. In making friends, when a casual acquaintance will suffice, we do not need to go deep. When attending a lecture, we can listen, but we do not have to delve deeply into the details of the research. Some academics act with humility and claim not to be so knowledgeable. In reality, those who make such claims are often deeply knowledgeable.

Dragons come from deep oceans, and fragrant orchids grow in the heart of the mountains. Important people usually live a secluded life. They think deeply about all matters so that they can make changes appropriately and respond well to all things, deep or shallow.

Some people say that the Dharma is too deep and difficult to understand. If you have not swum in the flowing Ganges River,

how can you find out how deep it is? When propagating the Dharma, Dharma water can flow to all the continents because, whether it is shallow or deep, it can explain the truth of every situation. It can prescribe the right medication for every sickness. When an elephant, a horse and a rabbit cross a river, the marks they make are different; but the depth of the river remains the same. People who understand this concept will declare, "The benefits I gain are deep. My good fortune is not at all shallow."

Everything has depth. This applies to water, people, reasoning, and even the Dharma. Deep oceans are for large ships to traverse, and provide a hiding place for big fish. Shallow water allows people to swim, dive and be purified. People who know how to drink and sing like to pace their drinking and croon in low tones. People learning to be teachers like to teach in ways that are simple and easy to understand. In farming, we have to cultivate deeply and plant shallowly. Friendships may be deep but the exchange of words should be shallow. We should go as deep or shallow as necessary, or be both at the same time.

MOUNTAINS AND OCEANS

According to an old Chinese saying, "The benevolent enjoy the mountains and the wise enjoy the water." Wealthy people mostly live up in the mountains, or near the waterfront. Therefore, mountains and oceans are closely related to people's lives, wealth, and recreation.

People like mountains because they can climb high and marvel at the magnificent views. In addition, there are trees, precious minerals, and all kinds of wildlife in the mountains. Some people are willing to sacrifice themselves just to climb the highest peaks. High mountains also nourish people's morals, personalities, cultivation, and willpower. When people praise others for their character, they often say it is "as high as the mountains."

While many people like mountains, others prefer the ocean. The ocean offers endless horizons, and beaches are great for taking long walks. We can observe seagulls flying and fish swimming in the water. Moreover, there are treasures deep in the ocean, such as coral reefs and energy resources. Some people risked their lives and gave up careers to sail the oceans. Although a few discovered new continents or islands, many ended up losing their lives.

What does the world have that are the most, the largest, the highest, and the deepest? They are the mountains and the oceans. A poem from the Tang Dynasty says, "Three parts mountain, six parts water, one part field." This means that mountains make up thirty percent of the earth, water is sixty percent, and the flat land available for humans only ten percent.

People who depend on mountains for a living use its woods and produce, and hunt there. Those who rely on the oceans to survive are often involved in salt making, sea products, and fishing.

Mountains and oceans change endlessly and are unpredictable. Mountains can help us accomplish our goals but can also ruin our lives. Similarly, the oceans can provide us with wealth or take away our lives. Some people say our gratitude for the love and care of our parents is higher than mountains and deeper than the ocean. This illustrates how difficult it is for us to repay them.

It is lonely and cold high up in the mountains, and difficult to negotiate the terrain deep in the oceans. High mountains and deep oceans are like the ups and downs in life. How do we balance life in the world between the mountains and the oceans?

Though mountains and oceans can provide us with recreation and relaxation, they are not the best places to reside for a long time. We should live amidst people in populated areas, such as in towns and cities, in order to create social benefits together. We can take vacations in the mountains or oceans from time to time, but should not live there permanently. Although we can benefit and become wise from the mountains and oceans, our society and country are still in need of many courageous people!

PLAIN WATER

Due to differences in location and ethnicity, people around the world have different types of diets. For instance, Asians eat a diet based on rice or noodles, and others on meat or vegetables and grains. Many Westerners seem to prefer bread, milk, and salads.

While different people eat different types of food, what they all share in common is a need for water, because water sustains life. Historically, people started out drinking plain water and progressed to tea, coffee, juice, and soft drinks. These beverages supply people of different lifestyles with the refreshment they need.

Water is equally important for everyone, whether he/she comes from nobility or poverty. We all drink a certain amount of water everyday. The water we drink may come from a bottle, a filter, or the tap, or be taken directly out of rivers and mountain streams for free.

There is a saying, "merit is like water," which means that as soon as we use it up, our merit or water is gone. Therefore, many elders often admonish younger generations to "treasure a drop of water like gold."

Buddhism often uses water as an analogy for the Dharma. Water can nourish, cleanse, and moisturize. Similarly, the Dharma can nourish faith, moisturize our body and mind, and cleanse us of our unwholesomeness. While the Dharma is the truth, when we compare it to water, water is just as important as the truth. A drop of water provides an opportunity for life. Drinking a glass of plain water every day costs next to nothing, but it is very important in sustaining life. So while plain water is bland and tasteless, we cannot live a day without it. When we have visitors, a glass of plain water is often enough to show our sincerity. In the past, many poor scholars could only afford a simple note as a gift, so if a poor family offered a glass of water, it expressed endless hospitality. People often supplied free refreshment to weary travelers in the form of plain water. Today, bottled water is practical and necessary, and a most precious relief for victims of natural disasters or even participants in activities and functions.

Plain water is the original taste of life. Sometimes a glass of water can cure many ills. When we have plenty of water, we fail to appreciate its value; we suffer beyond words when there is a shortage.

Some Middle Eastern countries have to import water from abroad for their citizens. It is even more expensive than the oil they produce. The United States is a big country, but many of its desert areas are still undeveloped due to a lack of water. While Americans enjoy advanced technology, they look at these endless deserts and feel helpless.

Traditional Buddhist temples designate a monk to be the "Water Charge," a person who looks after the water. The 'water charge' needs to make good use of water resources and not waste them. Since ancient times, Buddhism has placed much emphasis on protecting the natural environment, ecosystems and resources, because even a drop of water must be well preserved and not wasted.

"The friendship between the wise is as bland as water." Water consists of simple components and most beverages need water in order to blend and mix well. Therefore, water has a harmonizing function. In addition, it is also an antiseptic and purifying agent. Drinking water is boiled and endures high temperatures in order to become drinkable, just as people need to be tested before they become useful.

CLIMATE AND WEATHER

What changes most in the world is probably the weather. It can be unpredictably warm or cold. The temperature, sunshine, and rainfall can be completely different in the northern and southern parts of the same country. Even within the same region, there can be multiple types of weather. In Australia, for instance, the city of Melbourne is known for experiencing four seasons in a single day.

Geographical location is the main reason for different types of climates. There are warm, mild, and polar regions. Regardless of the location and climate, people live in all these places. Just as Chan masters say, "Go to cold places when it is cold, and warm places when it is hot." Hot or cold, there is no place to hide from the climate. We must face it and adapt ourselves because that is the best way to deal with it.

With advances in technology, there are now central heating systems in some extremely cold regions, as well as traditional clay or brick beds with a small fire burning underneath to keep us warm. In warm or hot areas, people try to stay cool under the shade of trees or use swamp coolers to lower the temperature. Many people now use air conditioning.

Climate also varies with the type of terrain: continental, oceanic, desert, mountain, and prairie. However, changes in the weather cannot compare to how fast people change moods. Like the weather, we change every hour, minute, and second of our lives. We may meet someone who is gentle like a spring breeze. Another may be cold and indifferent like the winds in late fall. Others may have mood swings, unstable emotions, and a poor temper. We can describe them as being "cloudy, with sunshine and occasional showers."

The weather outside affects us physically, making us feel warm or cold. The weather inside us influences our emotions, and others have to detect which season we are in from our emotional responses at the moment.

Climate and weather play a major role in shaping a country's culture. For instance, people who live in warm regions tend not to

do a lot of physical labor at a fast pace but instead prefer to take it easy, due to the high temperatures. They tend to put on weight and are more listless. Their thoughts are more developed. On the other hand, people who live in cold climates find it easier to cultivate the spirit of perseverance and diligence and are better able to endure hardships.

Food rots easily in warm weather and can be kept for longer periods of time when it is cold. In cold places, even animals and plants are more resilient. Old pines and green cypresses all go through the baptism of extreme cold weather. However, "when it gets so hot that people sweat, even the centers of the flowers in the lotus pond are fragrant." Heat can often temper the essence within. Therefore, be it hot or cold, if we can adapt well, we are capable.

In daily life, some people prefer the weather to be spring-like all year, neither warm nor cold. Other people feel that a simple life without changes is not challenging enough. In reality, places where seasonal changes are distinct, with warm spring breezes, hot summer days, chilly autumn frosts, and cold winter snow, are more like people. Some people are warm like spring, passionate like summer, solemn and cool like autumn, and wooden and cold like winter.

What is the most likeable weather? What personality should a person have in order to be more acceptable to everyone? Can we learn from the way the weather changes?

SHIPS AND BOATS

Ships have enabled humans to conquer seventy-eight percent of the world's surface. People built ships to realize their ambition to overcome flowing rivers and oceans. Since their invention ships and boats have become closely linked to the lives of humans.

People relied on ships to discover a new continent, to look for treasures deep in the oceans, and to cruise around the world. The West was able to conquer Asia because of ships. During the Epoch of the Three Kingdoms, Zhuge Liang, renowned strategist of his time, used straw boats to collect numerous arrows from the enemy as weapons, outwitting his rivals in the kingdom.

There are many examples of ships as metaphors. People in an organization encourage its members to cooperate well and to help one another by reminding them they are "all in the same boat." If we fall into bad company or make investment mistakes, we say we "have boarded the pirate ship." When our affairs take an unforeseen turn, it is like "a boat overturning in a sewer." When we see how difficult it is for a couple to come together as husband and wife, we say, "It takes ten years of cultivation to ride in the same boat, and a hundred to sleep in the same bed." We describe life with all its difficulties and uncertainties as "a boat on the vast ocean."

We encourage students by telling them that learning is like rowing a boat upstream. We wish others smooth sailing as a blessing for career and travel. In love, some people "step on two boats at the same time," meaning they have more than one love interest. When describing people's determination in what they do, "destroying the cooking pots and scuttling the ship" means they cannot turn back. Those who are especially magnanimous are considered to have "the tummy of a minister, large enough to row a boat in." For matters that we cannot change, we offer the excuse that "the ship will be straight when it docks." The compassion of bodhisattvas toward sentient beings is described as "the boat of

loving kindness going in reverse."

Throughout history, boats and ships have been an important means of transportation. Therefore, they have become a metaphor for poets to express the sorrow of departure and homesickness. For instance, Shi Renzhang of the Chin Dynasty wrote, "the homecoming boat at the end of the year is light; tears roll down when the singing and dancing are over." Su Shi of the Song Dynasty pined, "the loveless water of the Bian River flows east, carrying a boatload of parting sorrow toward the West." In addition, Xunzi, a contemporary of Mencius, compared the relationship between a political leader and the general public to a boat and water, meaning that the public can support their political rulers and also overthrow them.

In Buddhism, a ship symbolizes being saved and the ability to reach the other shore. The Dharma is like a boat for us to traverse the river of living and dying. In the Tolerance Sutra, it says, "Tolerance is a large boat to take us through hardships." The Sixth Patriarch relied on his master to row him away in a boat. Thus, the famous verse, "In delusion, we need a teacher to help us across; in enlightenment, we get across ourselves."

Boats can also be home to many people, such as Amsterdam's houseboats. In Bangkok, boats are not only homes but also mobile stalls for goods. They form the "floating market," which is truly amazing to those who live on the land. Today, some people choose to live in houseboats after they retire, whereas fishermen and some refugees can only live in boats. Cruise ships are used for entertainment, and many yachts are used for racing.

We should be like boats, which protect people as they cross over rushing waters to the other shore. We should be able to carry all things and serve as a means of reliance, helping to save people in the ocean of suffering by providing them with hope.

Are you willing to be a boat?

WATER AND FIRE

When people get along very well with one another, we say they are as harmonious as water and milk. Otherwise, they are like water and fire, not at all compatible. Water and fire are generally considered mutually destructive. However, in Taiwan, there is a ridge that is the source of both water and fire, which illustrates that water and fire can be mutually tolerant.

In the midst of hard frozen ice, there is still warmth. That is fire. And deep under icy land, there can be hot springs. In the middle of a hot raging fire, there is moisture. When water boils, it embraces the element of fire. Water and fire may be mutually destructive, because water can put out fire and fire can turn water into steam and clouds, but they can also be mutually tolerant.

Nothing in the world can exist on its own, solely because of its strength or size. Even things as hard as brass and iron can be forged into steel by fire. Water is soft and fluid, yet it can support heavy vessels. People who are strong by nature can be overcome by gentle ways. Therefore, everything in the world competes with and supports each other at the same time. When all things can tolerate one another, they can exist together. If objects can do this, why do people have so many problems coexisting?

A country needs scholars as well as soldiers. Society requires the support of farmers, workers, merchants, and all other professionals. A company must have people to plan its strategies and people to carry them out. In a family, the personalities of its members may vary, some quiet and others active. However, in spite of differences in personality, they must respect and love one another, admiring each other's characteristics. As they work according to their interests, life will be so much more interesting and colorful. On the contrary, if everyone is arrogant and conceited and looks down on each other, boycotting each other's efforts, it will be like the intolerance of water and fire. How can a country and a society exist in harmony then?

Buddhism teaches that the four elements of earth, water, fire, and wind are empty in nature. They must be mutually tolerant in order to survive. For instance, when the four elements of the

human body are in harmony, the individual will enjoy good health. When rain and wind are timely between heaven and earth, people will enjoy a bumper harvest. If the amount of warmth and water are right, plants will bloom and bear fruit. These all illustrate how the four elements of earth, water, fire and wind are mutually tolerant.

Today, countries cannot tolerate one another, different groups fail to cooperate with each other, people find it impossible to get along, religions do not have mutual respect, and races continue to discriminate against one another. They are being mutually destructive, like fire and water. It is against the law of nature. When people cannot tolerate others, they are seeking their own destruction.

The world did not come into being because of one cause or condition. It exists due to many interconnected and interdependent causes and conditions. It is like the coexistence of the eyes, ears, nose, tongue, and body, which allows a person to be healthy and wholesome; if any one of them is missing, a person is handicapped and incomplete.

In recent studies, more and more scientists have discovered that the largest reserve of energy may exist deep in the oceans. The bottom of the ocean is icy cold, yet it is hot enough to melt the ice and allow methane hydrate to exist in crystalline form. The heat created by the coldness of ice shows how water and fire can be mutually tolerant. If water and fire can be mutually tolerant, why then can't the differences in interests, characteristics, cultures, ethnicities, and religions of humans be the same?

LISTEN, CONTEMPLATE AND CULTIVATE

When someone praises us, does it make us feel happy? Have we ever considered whether it was justified? When someone slanders us, do we feel upset? Have we ever considered it reasonable or unreasonable? When we hear others talk or when we think of something, do we give it serious consideration before acting upon it? Even though we should think and react quickly, doing things without thinking is often inappropriate.

Some people are attached to their views and do not accept the benevolent words of others. If they hear them and do not give consideration to what others have to say, they cannot accomplish the best results in what they undertake. Buddhism recommends that people approach this basic human flaw by "listening, contemplating, and cultivating." This can help us enter into samadhi, or meditative concentration. By listening, contemplating and cultivating, we can achieve wisdom. And we can only reach our goals by going through each stage of listening, contemplating and cultivating. Confucianism teaches, "Learning without contemplating is crooked. Contemplating without learning is dangerous." This describes the importance of listening, contemplating, and cultivating.

Real listening means listening attentively when others speak. Do you listen to the entirety of what someone says? If you hear biased speech, do you listen to other sources? Bodhisattvas cultivate the twenty-five perfections. Perfection in listening is an important practice. Buddhism emphasizes learning through listening. Listening is more important than seeing with our own eyes. Even though we cannot see clearly from afar, we are able to hear from a distance. We are not able to see what things were like in the past, but we can still listen to others speak about it. We cannot see who is talking next door, but we can hear them. In learning to listen, we should know how to listen, and listen well. When we can hear the "sound of no sound," then we have achieved the wisdom of listening.

In contemplating, we have to contemplate correctly, purely, and carefully. We should always think three times before we act. Those who are wealthy may be valuable, but those who have the ability to think are not only valuable, they are far more respectable. Philosophers unravel the phenomena of the universe through their thinking. Scientists invent technology by thinking and experimenting. Writers produce beautiful literature by contemplating extensively. If we are able to think, reflect and contemplate, then we have achieved the wisdom of contemplating.

Cultivating is to uphold and actualize. In cultivating, we can cultivate asceticism with joy: truthfully, internally, with others, or on our own. When our clothes are torn, we need to mend them. When our house needs repairs, we fix it. When our body and mind are in bad shape, we need to revitalize ourselves. As long as we are willing to take the first step, why worry about not being able to reach the end of the long path? If we are prepared to take action, why worry about not being able to succeed in a protracted enterprise? By cultivating our behavior, we can gain perfection in being human. By cultivating our minds, we can achieve Buddhahood. As long as we cultivate, we can achieve the wisdom of cultivation.

Therefore, Buddhism encourages us to listen, contemplate, and cultivate in order to achieve samadhi.

MORNING AND EVENING PRACTICE

Many people have some sort of morning and evening practice. Practice is necessary for success in whatever we do: for good health and for giving meaning and stability to our lives.

In addition to the homework assigned by their teachers, hardworking students have their morning recitation and evening review of what they have learned in school. These are the morning and evening practices of students.

Politicians and entrepreneurs often hold morning meetings, speak on the phone, meet with guests, and dictate letters to their secretaries, always getting work done in the morning. In the evening, they read documents, have discussions, and/or hold dinner meetings. This is the evening practice of politicians and entrepreneurs.

Faith practitioners get up early in the morning and recite a prayer and worship as a commitment and devotion to their religion. Before they go to bed, they meditate or pray as their evening practice.

In Buddhist temples, the bell and drum are sounded every morning and every evening all year round. Monastics take their morning and evening practice very seriously. If they practice every morning and evening, their character improves, bringing a higher level of transcendence to their lives.

Most of the time we busy ourselves for the sake of others, work on our careers, or labor extra hours to make money. In the end, everything that we work so hard for may not be ours. There is a saying: "We cannot take anything with us when we leave the world except for our karma, which follows us everywhere." The merits that we have accumulated benefit us in this life and are also available for us to enjoy in future lives. So why don't we spare some time every day just for ourselves?

Today, people schedule out the entire day, the next day, and even the next month and upcoming year. Everything is set out in their planners. For those who plan their lives so thoroughly, they should also set aside time for morning and evening practice. Staying in bed for hours, being lazy, and watching television are

not the best morning practices; nor are formal dinner parties, drinking in bars, and dancing the best evening practices.

We should consider how Zeng Shen, a disciple of Confucius, practiced "Reflecting on myself and my actions three times a day," or how Yuan Liaofan, a devout Buddhist practitioner during the Ming Dynasty, recorded his own faults and merits daily. There are many scholars and powerful business people who read in the morning and write in the evening, learn a foreign language, practice calligraphy, or study and contemplate the mottoes of the wise. They all have their own morning and evening practices.

We should make use of the time in the morning, when our minds are clear and we feel good physically and spiritually, to recite a sutra, read a book, learn a new language, and make plans. In the evening, we should reflect, review, and record what we did during the day. At the same time, we should also plan and develop our future work. The evening is wonderful.

We all should establish our own morning and evening practices. They are not the monopoly of students and religious leaders.

MEAL TIME

In today's society, every minute counts, so some people eat their meals while they work. For instance, supervisors eat breakfast as they listen to their secretaries give them an account of the day's activities: what clients they will meet, the meetings they will attend, documents to read, and calls to return. During this time, they also assign work to their secretaries. During lunch they entertain clients or make deals on the phone. Even though the evening meal may be the only time available to share with family or good friends, some people still do not stop working. Therefore, many entrepreneurs and business people often end their conversations during the day with, "See you at lunch." or "We'll talk again over dinner."

When work does not stop during mealtimes, especially over breakfast, the never-ending stream of contacts and discussions often affect the emotions of the individual. The good news or troubles that the reports may bring influence people's moods. If something is really distressing, a person may not be able to eat, and for some, a call with unwelcome news may get them down for the rest of the day.

When problems are resolved over breakfast, many people feel relaxed and the day seems easy. Similarly, lunch is enjoyable if one is caught up with his or her work. Otherwise, eating lunch is a burden, knowing that much still needs to be resolved afterwards.

Dinner is the time for family members to share their love and support. When people laugh and joke at the dinner table, it is far more enjoyable than making money or getting a promotion. However, when family members do not get along or if someone chooses to share only troubles, then the home environment will be thick with tension and stress. No wonder some people prefer to stay out late and avoid going home for dinner.

Most people today keep a very hectic schedule and think that they have no choice but to make use of mealtime to get work done. Because phone calls and newspapers accompany breakfast, their emotions are driven by the ups and downs of the day's news.

While lunch should provide a needed break, they may find it difficult to enjoy because of work, gossip, and problems. Dinner may also be spoiled by family bickering, which can cause indigestion or even ulcers.

We should eat every meal with pleasure, in proper portions, and during a fixed time. However, people today eat with a burdened mind and at irregular times. In addition, the food may be unhealthy, loaded with salt or too many hot spices, which can harm the heart and kidneys. This is not the way to maintain one's health.

Buddhism teaches, "Morning porridge has ten benefits, lunch is delicious and wonderful, and dinner should be contemplated as medicine." This is the healthy way to eat. Additionally, we should not overeat; we should only let ourselves get about seventy percent full and then go for a walk afterwards. We should eat well at breakfast, have a full lunch, and only take a light dinner. These are all ways to eat healthily.

To maintain good health, we need to be vigilant at all times. Mealtime is an important part of this regimen. We must take it seriously!

WORK TIME

In societies around the world, most people go to work every-day. The concept of "nine to five" is commonly accepted as the norm for most workers around the globe. However, people can have different attitudes toward work, which can be classified as follows:

I. Taking work seriously

People who take their work seriously will review and/or sign documents, attend teleconferences and business meetings, engage in daily operations, and work in close conjunction with other people. They set and stick to a schedule, completing all necessary routine work by setting goals, delegating projects, evaluating business plans, prioritizing work activities, and preparing agendas and meeting minutes. Other duties may include delivering messages and/or giving directives to coworkers. Anything that needs to be resolved by a call or email is accomplished as required. Regardless of the situation, career-oriented people always utilize any means available to complete their tasks and meet project timelines. They are conscientious of their responsibilities and have regard for efficiency. Law-abiding and willing to serve, they are the serious and real workers.

In contrast, some people just get by at work, putting in hours but not being productive. Although they hold impressive titles and high status, playing important roles within the corporation, they only pretend to work. They are irresponsible and inattentive in dealing with daily operations, spending most of their time putting up appearances. The decisions they make only benefit themselves, making it difficult for others. They are attached to their views and make it their mission to give others a hard time. During work hours they gossip, make personal calls to their friends, and run private errands. When it is time to go, they are the first to leave. Worse yet, they seek every opportunity to line their pockets on business trips and charge the company for overtime while conducting personal affairs. They are only faking work.

II. Killing Time

Some people go to work and leave on time. Although they

appear to be energetic, and seem to take their jobs seriously, in reality they spend their time leisurely drinking coffee or tea, reading the newspaper or their favorite books, doodling, making personal calls, taking breaks to gossip, knitting, watching television, playing video games, or getting on the Internet to chat online. Some snack during work hours or take long breaks to shop for daily necessities and groceries. This type of worker is not efficient, and basically comes to work only to kill time. For them, the workplace is for socializing, coordinating personal affairs, and planning vacations.

III. Double-dipping

Some people take advantage of their work hours to gain personal profits. They write articles, go online in search of information to earn extra money, monitor their investments on the stock market, and use the company phone to conduct personal business. These workers "double-dip." For them, work is a cover-up to make use of company assets to operate personal businesses.

Some people compare the relationship between workers and their bosses to a cat and mouse. When the cat is away, the mouse goes anywhere and does anything it pleases. However, for conscientious workers, whether their bosses or the cat are there or not, they work according to their conscience, ethics, and values. These are the distinguished workers. Therefore, those who work should know what is the right attitude to have in the workplace, and society will certainly improve as a whole.

FINDING FLAVOR IN THE FLAVORLESS

Every dish has a different flavor-some have too much seasoning and some not quite enough. Each has its own taste. Peas and carrots may be bland, but they have a simple flavor that most people enjoy.

The flavor of human sentiments also varies, from the very passionate to the very cold. While some people are warm toward their friends, others are less than enthusiastic in their relationships. However, a friendship that is heavy on passion and intimacy will deteriorate over time and become a thing of the past. On the other hand, many intelligent people, while treasuring their friends' intelligence, prefer personal relationships to be as bland as water. They choose to build friendships based on respect, appreciation, integrity, and righteousness. They will sacrifice their lives for their friends and share their fate and suffering. As a result, they are able to foster solid friendships.

Water has the uncanny ability to blend well with any flavor because it is odorless. It is unlike the blend of salt and sugar, where the two ingredients do not agree well with one another to create flavor. Therefore, flavorlessness is a flavor that transcends any other. Most people are attracted to what is sweet and fragrant, and consider blandness to be too plain and thus deficient. What they have overlooked is that flavorlessness has its own flavor. A perfume must be mild and pleasant for its scent to last. The smell of a flower can be too strong to delight the senses. Although the peony is a symbol of wealth and prosperity, it is not as appealing as an orchid, with its hint of sweetness that compares to the temperament of a benevolent person. The most beautiful woman in the world needs only a little make up to bring out her beauty, for a heavily powdered face will only serve to make her look cheap.

An ordinary life is not without interest, because simplicity is not without quality. It is like the simple elegance of jade, or the tranquil life of a person who is unmoved by fame, power, and fortune. It is a way of life that differs from one that emphasizes passion and affection. Although some people find happiness in wealth and prosperity, others are content to live in anonymity, far from the hustle and bustle of a big city.

When Ksitigarbha Bodhisattva's attendant grew weary of the

lonely mountain life, he desperately wanted to leave and rid himself of loneliness. Although the Bodhisattva was not prepared to let his attendant go, he had no other choice but to see him off with a poem: "Homesickness has befallen you because of loneliness on the path to enlightenment. You have politely asked to leave the clouds and mountains to return to the secular way of life. As you take a drink from the stream, do not chase after the reflection of the moon. As you make a cup of tea, do not dwell too long on the beauty of the flowers. When you are ready to leave my side, do not shed a tear of worry, for I will always have the clouds and sunsets as my constant companions." Most eminent masters of the past acquired a sense of simplicity at a very young age, and learned to look for the meaning of life in blandness.

Famous philosopher Cheng Yi of the Song Dynasty once composed a poem to describe the carefree nature of a spring day: "With a gentle breeze and cloudless sky, noon is just around the corner. As I stroll leisurely past the stream and flowers, people mistake the happiness in my heart for a young man's idleness." Although there is nothing wrong with wanting simplicity in our lives, we cannot be flavorless in our ways. For example, our conversations would be dull and uninteresting if they were without substance and content. So flavorlessness is a deficiency that must be overcome. We must learn to find flavor in the flavorless in order to acquire the ultimate taste. For example, the more we chew life's green olive, the more flavor there is.

If we are to truly appreciate the taste of philosophical truths, we must savor them slowly. In order to fully understand the Buddhist concepts of loving-kindness, compassion, magnanimity and selflessness, we must realize them gradually. Although the practice of meditation and paying homage to the Buddha may seem simple and plain, they are the source of infinite Dharma joy; if we practice wholeheartedly, they acquire a different flavor.

We must learn not to season things too heavily or use excessive oil, salt and sugar when we prepare our meals; otherwise we will ruin our appetite. We must regard blandness as the best flavor for our food, because it improves and extends our health. Blandness is the original flavor of all things, including life.

BEFORE GOING TO WORK

Since more than half of every country's population works for a living, special care should be given to the welfare of working people.

Since every company has its own policies regarding the conduct of its employees during business hours, we should focus our attention on the hours before work. If our jobs require us to be at work no later than 9:00 a.m., we should get up by at least 7:00 a.m. What should we do with the two hours that are available to us? Below is a list of activities that we can do before we go to work:

I. 20 minutes for washing and cleaning ourselves:
When we bathe and brush our teeth in the morning, we are doing something that is second nature. Therefore, we can use these twenty minutes to mentally review what we should do during the day, including important tasks and appointments; otherwise, we may forget them and be criticized for being forgetful.

II. 10 minutes for morning practice:
We can then offer incense, fresh flowers or a cup of clean water to the buddhas and the bodhisattvas. There is no need for us to be fancy or elaborate. We can just choose one of the three offerings. After paying homage to the Buddhas and the bodhisattvas, we can recite one of the "*Pearls of Wisdom - Prayers for Engaged Living*" or the "Heart Sutra" once. We can also meditate for five minutes, chant the Amitabha Buddha's name ten times, or practice the Buddha's Light Meditation Method, paying homage to the Buddhas and the bodhisattvas.

III. 30 minutes for morning exercise:
We can jog in place, walk around the yard, or do stretching exercises.

IV. 30 minutes for breakfast and chores:
Every family member should be at the breakfast table for the first meal of the day. Eating breakfast is like a family meeting, where everyone is present to share his/her plans for the day and to praise and appreciate one another's efforts. Although everybody

eats at a different pace, we should at least devote
twenty minutes of our time to household chores, such as
washing the dishes, watering the plants or simply cleaning
our rooms. Afterwards, we should get ready for work.

VI. At least 30 minutes for commute time:
If our means of transportation is the train, bus or subway, we
can use this time to read a book or newspaper. If we drive to
work, we can turn on the radio and listen to the news while
fighting the morning traffic. However, if we ride a bicycle,
we must be very careful of the cars around us. It really does
not matter how we get to work, so long as we can arrive in
time to socialize with our co-workers and greet our bosses
properly.

In addition to allowing ourselves at least two hours to get
ready for work, we must also be very conscious of our attitude,
clothes and demeanor so that we fit in at work. Our manners must
be dignified and poised, and our energy level must be high and
enthusiastic. We should always smile and be pleasant when inter-
acting with people. When it is time to work, we must put forth our
best effort and maintain good work habits. We must take initiative
and never refuse a job that is assigned to us, in addition to being
diligent, logical, and energetic. We must be forthright and flaw-
less in our planning, and always be ready to report to our superiors on our progress. If we can do the work of several people, and
have the appreciation and acknowledgement of our supervisors,
our future will be bright and promising.

IDLE TALK

Idle talk is so named because it is often nonsense, empty words, lies, or even dirty talk, gossip and slander. Idle speech can plant the cause of life-long hatred between good friends. A bit of hatred seemingly harmless nonsense can create endless trouble, and a word of gossip can ruin many years of a cordial relationship between coworkers. Empty words allow others to see clearly what we are worth. A lie can lead others to despise our character and to scorn us as a person.

Ideally, the best speech is no speech! However, not saying anything is too passive. People should actively say positive words of kindness and compassion, and speak in praise of others. In addition, their speech should be helpful and encouraging.

After the September 11 attacks, many people became fearful of flying. When a woman had to wait over two hours for a delayed flight, she became frustrated and worried that she might miss her important appointment. She complained openly, "Just let the plane be bombed!" The FBI later arrested her on account of a perceived threat, and the airline filed a case against her for the false report of a bomb. So the effect of idle talk can indeed be grave!

Some people enjoy making idle talk, which often brings unimaginable results. A maid working for the British royal family once bragged to a coworker in the kitchen, "I could easily poison the Queen's food and not be discovered." Her words spread. Although she claimed it was just idle talk, Buckingham Palace fired her for "very serious improper speech and behavior." She eventually went to jail, simply because of her careless words. Confucius said, "Speak not what is improper, see not what is improper, and listen not to what is improper." This is truly wise.

Generally speaking, some people tend to indulge in idle talk more than others. They spend time together, spreading gossip as they talk about anything that comes to mind. When we say too much, we tend not to think as much, so maybe people should spend more time thinking instead.

Some people today are wise and think before they speak, while others are foolish and think only after they speak. Thinking

and speaking should be in the right order. We should think before we speak, and only speak after we think well. More importantly, we should know when to speak, and remain quiet when appropriate.

The greatest evil in speech is saying meaningless words or claiming to know something that we know nothing about. However, the worst offense one can commit with speech is to slander others, especially by being insensitive. Some cold dishes may taste very good, but cold words are hard on the ears. Therefore, rather than engage in idle talk, we should speak more with truthfulness and integrity, and say things that are useful and constructive so that our speech is truly valuable.

LOVING WORDS

Speech is a tool people use to communicate with one another. There are different kinds of speech. Lies, harsh words, and idle or divisive talk all harm people. Only loving words are like a spring breeze and gentle showers, bringing life to earth.

Loving words consist of caring and supportive speech. They are respectful, friendly, and helpful. They should help others by giving confidence, offering support, and encouraging benevolent deeds. Everyone in the world likes loving speech. However, some are not using it well.

We can never speak enough loving words because "A loving word fills a room with fragrance." Loving words bring joy to everyone, like the perfume of flowers that permeates the air with its scent. It is like soft linen giving gentle care, or the sun spreading its warmth in.

When parents teach their children, teachers instruct their students, and seniors guide the younger generation, no matter what tone or words are used, they are all loving words. When senior officers speak loving words, their subordinates will certainly follow with joy, and when employers do so, their workers are perfectly willing to cooperate. Among parents, children and siblings, loving words should never cease. It is especially important between spouses, who should always speak loving words to please one another and to maintain a happy marriage, because loving words are the lubricant for constructive communication.

In reality, it is not always easy to say something that is appropriate for the occasion and acceptable to others. We take many exams in life, but oral tests seem to be the most important. Therefore, after babies are born, their parents teach them with the utmost patience. If we want to succeed in life, in addition to speaking the truth when dealing with others, loving words are the key to success.

Humble Table, Wise Fare says, "Leave behind the warm breeze of loving words, so that the whole world can be filled with the warmth of respect." If every member of a family speaks loving words, the family gains harmony and happiness. When each

person within an organization uses loving words, the organization will be harmonious. If the citizens of a country also speak loving words, unity can be achieved.

In learning a language, we need to speak with the elegance of literature and the contemplation of philosophy. Many people who do not read, study, or self-reflect often use tasteless or vulgar language. Therefore, we need to improve our language by reading, so that it can be filled with benevolence and kindness, giving joy to everyone.

Some people only speak in order to shock. In reality, if we do not know how to speak loving words we are better off not saying anything!

GRATUITIES

America is large and strong, and Americans are a proud and self-respecting people. They have the habit of tipping for services received. They will, for example, tip a baggage handler, a taxi driver, a waiter or waitress, or a maid. By contrast, Japan is not a very big nation, their homes are small, and giving gratuities is not a local custom, so establishments do not have the custom of receiving gratuities.

Although it is common to leave extra money for tips, we can also show gratitude with praise, a handshake, or a smile. As long as our gestures are sincere, our servers will gladly receive them without resentment. Since a gratuity can be perceived as a kind of reward, it is not limited to the service industry. This is true, for example, when we try to buy a new car and ask for extra incentives or discounts. It is like asking for tips.

Is a gratuity a good or bad thing? It can be undesirable when it gives rise to greed and petty advantages, but it is encouraged when it helps improve the quality of services. Since tips can be big or small, regardless of how large the bill is, a server must decide what kind of service he or she is willing to provide. In China, it used to be customary for waiters and waitresses to make a customer's tip known immediately after the customer paid the bill.

It is also fairly normal for Chinese people to repay a debt of gratitude with money. Patients will often express thanks with monetary gifts, but it is unethical for doctors to base the quality of treatment on the amount of the gratuity. Similarly, people in old China made a monetary offering upfront to the prospective teacher of their children as a symbol of respect; however, it would be immoral for teachers to sell themselves to the highest bidder and discriminate against those who are poor and disadvantaged.

Although it is common for us to reward good service with a good tip, giving a gratuity should be an art. We can, for example, conceal our tips in a handshake, or be discrete with our actions, and not appear boastful or demeaning. Since it is an act of gratitude, it should not be a burden to either the giver or the receiver.

However, some establishments have gone too far in their demands for service charges. Consider the following story: a man once went to a restaurant to see how he would be treated. After repeatedly testing the staff's patience and promptness of service, he was told by one of the waiters to just relax and enjoy his food, because he would be served well as long as he had not yet left the tip. When a gratuity has thus been abused and becomes an obligation, it is time to make an adjustment.

Although it is fairly common for people to tip their servers, different countries have different customs and rates. Places like India, Thailand, Nepal, Indonesia, China, the Philippines, Africa, and Europe all have different customs for giving and receiving gratuities. Before we visit a new place, we must take the time to understand their customs and "when in Rome, do as the Romans do."

Giving a gratuity is gratifying for both the giver and the receiver; the giver is pleased to reward good service with money, while the receiver is happy to earn extra income. Similarly, some animals like dolphins are much like their human counterparts. They enjoy receiving a reward when they give a special performance to entertain the audience. All in all, a gratuity is a good thing when it is given willingly and appropriately.

PAYING FEES

Students pay tuition fees for classes, while motorists pay parking fees. When we visit theme parks and other tourist attractions, or go to a movie, we have to pay for tickets. Buying an entrance ticket is paying a fee.

User fees are very common. For example, the construction, maintenance and employee salaries of any tourist attraction can cost a considerable amount of many. If no one pays these costs, how can the industry support itself? When tens of thousands of people pay to support a place or organization, the organization will surely be able to maintain or even improve its facilities and quality of service. On the other hand, when no one pays, the organization can only go down the path to bankruptcy. Therefore, charging a fee makes it possible for public facilities to grow and raise their standards.

In developed countries, paying a fee to hear a lecture, to watch a performance, or to use a public facility is taken for granted. Membership fees are required to join many groups and organizations. In addition, consumers have a duty to pay property and sales taxes. However, in developing countries people prefer to enjoy the amenities but not pay for them. This kind of thinking and behavior comes from getting things for free and is actually quite backward.

Paying fees is the key to social progress. It is like growing a pot of flowers. If we want the flowers to blossom beautifully for everyone to enjoy, we need to water and fertilize them. This is paying a fee. To watch dolphins perform, the audience buys tickets, which covers the cost of the fish the dolphins eat and the trainer who trains the dolphins, who are thereby indirectly paid for their performance. When we visit an observatory, we often look at the stars through a telescope. If we do not pay for this, where do the maintenance expenses come from?

When you drive from north to south on the freeways in Taiwan, you pass through nine tollbooths. In Japan, the toll fees required on the highways are usually even more expensive than the gas. It is through paying fees that investors accumulate suffi-

cient resources, a little at a time, to continue their operation. Fees are used not only to sustain the present facility but also to serve as the foundation for future improvements.

In reality, by giving others a kind word, a smile, a salute, a "thank you," or praise, we are connecting with them, which implies paying a fee also. While we do not have to pay for public property, such as sunshine or air, we should be charged to use other public or private amenities, such as national parks, art galleries, botanical gardens, and museums. When we go to a church or temple and make a donation, are we not paying a fee there as well?

Paying fees is a crucial way to support the enormous expenses of organizations. Those paying should be perfectly willing to do so, because it is a matter of course, since there are no free lunches. The fee system should be used extensively around the world. If we consider the payment of fees the same as making a donation, we embrace a positive attitude.

PENETRATING SPACE

"A tiny crack can burst a dam; a small dispute can ruin a friendship." Minor issues may not attract attention. However, some issues are powerful in their ability to penetrate and may result in major devastation if they are not fixed immediately. Water, air, germs, and viruses can enter any place. According to a saying, "Good things do not get published, yet bad happenings can spread for a thousand miles." Rumors and unwholesome deeds can penetrate even further and wider. Space is the condition that enables penetration, since everything needs space.

There was once an apprentice who was full of confidence, thinking he had completed his learning. As he bade his master farewell, his master took a cup filled with rocks and asked, "Is it full?" The apprentice replied: "Yes, Master." The master grabbed a bunch of small pebbles and put them in the cup and asked again, "Is it full?" "It is, Master," replied the apprentice. The master put a handful of sand in the cup and asked, "Is it full?" The apprentice exclaimed, "Yes!" Finally, the master poured a bowl of water into the cup and asked the same question. The student was speechless.

Where there is a crack, air enters. Where there is negligence, wealth is lost. Our bad habits, erroneous thoughts, and unwholesome intentions also penetrate everything. However, people have become accustomed to this, and due to a lack of awareness are conquered without even realizing it. It is said: "Living with good people is like entering a room full of orchids. The fragrance can no longer be detected over time. Being with bad people is like entering a fish market; over time we no longer notice the foul smell."

To prevent penetration, things should be airtight so that nothing can enter, not even through a pinhole. If we are afraid that our shortcomings may become exposed, the best remedy is to cultivate. By cultivating ourselves broadly, we can increase our strength. Evil can only penetrate when we are weak and unsure. If we are solid and firm like an iron ball, no poison can infiltrate.

Our faces have seven openings. If any of the openings are clogged, we get sick and perhaps contract a fatal illness. Windows

are openings for fresh air, but they may make us sick if they are too big and left open when the temperature changes. When people have a big mouth and say too much or speak without thinking, it can cause trouble.

Openings can be good or bad. Woodwind instruments like the clarinet or the Chinese flute cannot make music without holes. Kettles and pressure cookers explode if there are no openings to let out steam and pressure. It is important to have drain holes in ditches to let dirty water escape. Therefore, holes and openings must be used well in order to benefit us. However, when there are a hundred holes and a thousand sores, the situation has deteriorated beyond rescue. If both of our nostrils are clogged, we can die.

When used well, needle cameras are positive scientific devices to preserve time and history. If they are used negatively, they become weapons of crime, prying into the privacy of others. Therefore, everything in this world can be good or bad. It is all relative. Science is the same. It is important to use scientific inventions positively to help humanity, or better still, in accord with the teachings of the Dharma. Technology can accomplish more than providing a convenience or benefit to humankind; it may someday help us to realize world peace.

THE INSPIRATION OF SHOES

Feet are for walking and serve a very important purpose. In order to protect them, people invented shoes. Shoes are made of various materials for different occasions. There are wooden clogs, casual slippers, leather shoes, straw shoes, sneakers, boots, ice skates, rock climbing shoes, and sandals.

When we put on shoes, they not only keep us warm but also complement our appearance. The wife of the former president of the Philippines, Imelda Marcos, had a collection of over a thousand pairs of shoes to show off her exceptional wealth and status. This exemplifies the difference between the rich and the poor. While the wealthy collect shoes as a hobby, the poor cannot even afford a single pair. In the old days in China, when farming was the common means of livelihood, many children longed to own a pair of shoes but often grew up without ever having any. Though many grew up bare foot, they learned to treasure things and to cultivate the virtues of gratitude and contentment.

Once there was a man who bemoaned his poverty because he could not afford any shoes. Then he met a handicapped man who had no feet, and he was grateful for being able-bodied. This illustrates that we are often worse off than some but better off than others.

In the Iranian movie, the "*Children of Heaven*," the leading actor ran a race and won first place. Surprisingly, he wept, "I don't want first place. I only need third place." By winning third place he could have won a pair of shoes for his little sister. It is a very moving story that usually moves audiences to tears.

Buddhist monastics wear "Lohan" shoes with six openings, signifying the diligent practice of the Six Perfections by every practitioner. The openings also mean that we need to see through the impermanence of the world's phenomena, as the following saying suggests, "As we take off our shoes for bed, we don't know if tomorrow will come." Because of the impermanence of life, we should uphold right views and make good use of every moment to cultivate with diligence.

Although shoes protect our feet, they can also be a form of

restraint. Therefore, taking our shoes off is like putting down a heavy load. As we release the worries in our mind and follow circumstances, we can be at ease. On the other hand, it is important to watch our step. We should keep both feet firmly on the ground every step of the way, making a footprint with every step we take. We create our own paths in life. Therefore, we should be steady on our feet in order to do well. By being stable and steadfast, we can walk on a bright path toward our future.

DISCOUNTING

Discounting is one of the ways businesses promote sales. By giving a discount off the original price, both vendor and customer are happy because they are willing to make a deal, especially when the buyer gets something he/she wants at a lower price. Discounts do not mean much though; they are really a type of sales gimmick. Businesses make use of consumer greed to acquire small gains by discounting, so they have become increasingly popular in the commercial world.

In addition to discounts in business, in our daily lives as workers many people have discounts on their minds. In the workplace, some employees think that it is not necessary to put forth all their effort, and feel satisfied with giving just seventy or eighty percent. When it comes to the difficulty and duration of a job, people sometimes try to take advantage by working fewer hours or reducing the workload to gain small "discounts" for themselves. People who like to get discounts in what they do may appear to be gaining an advantage; however, in the eyes of their employers, it is the character of these workers that has really been discounted.

Some people strive to be the best, fastest, truest, or even most perfect in what they do. They try to exhibit their best spirit and loyalty. Other people just try to get by. Even without the judgment of their supervisors, these people should be able to tell immediately who the winners and losers are.

Whether anything in the world is valuable or not depends on how useful and necessary it is. For things that are of use, their value is certainly above their price, but for things that we do not need, then no matter how much they are discounted, what good will they do us? Therefore, we need not be greedy over small gains, but we should be clear on the value of usefulness. When we speak, what we say should be of value. Otherwise, others will not take us seriously. Our every action should be carried out properly; then our actions will be invaluable. By being pretentious, stiff and unnatural, others will not value us. A true and sincere smile and wise thinking are also of high value. The value of

something depends on whether we can recognize its value or not. It should not be assessed by how much of a discount there is.

A multi-billionaire may be wealthier than a nation, but if people dislike him/her for having poor ethics, he/she is ethically valueless. People who are good at making connections with others are welcome everywhere they go; being materially poor does not diminish their good will. Their value is not judged by economics, because they have a highly valued and noble character.

In assessing the value of a country, a society, an individual or ourselves, do we really need to calculate discounts?

CARS

Humans walk with their feet, but prefer the convenience of a bicycle or motorbike for distance a few miles away. However, a motorcycle, with its two wheels and capability for high speeds, can be very dangerous. A car is safer. Domestic models have less appeal for some people because their styling and engines are not as good as those of imports, especially luxury cars such as Mercedes Benz and BMW. These are fancy and prestigious to drive!

People who do not own a car admire those who do. When we own a car though, we worry about parking, burglary, vandalism, expenses, and accidents. At one time, people who owned expensive import cars were targets of carjacking and kidnapping. In the end, the anxiety can be too much to bear, and some people sell such cars. Returning to car-less days makes life so much easier.

Cars are used mainly for commuting and transporting goods; they have advantages and disadvantages. They require maintenance, a parking space, and gasoline. Many people compare their cars and are preoccupied with whose car is better or worse. Though owning a car provides convenience, it brings worries as well, and if it breaks down in the middle of the road it can cause endless frustration! While cars can be obstacles at times, when driven improperly, they can also cause accidents and bring harm to people.

However, cars are an important means of transportation and can raise the quality of life for modern people. They can be used as mobile schools, providing time and space to increase our knowledge of many subjects, such as history, geography, and the humanities. Cars are the product of progress, shortening the time and space between people; they are a necessity of life. We should not buy cars for vanity or just for joy rides. We should especially never drive when drinking. Many young people like to take their friends for a ride after they have been drinking and often end up ruining their lives.

Passengers should also know proper etiquette. For instance, everyone should wear a seat belt. When getting in a car, the

young should sit in the back, and when getting out, seniors should be helped out first. When driving we should follow traffic laws, pay attention to who has the right of way, stoplights, and pedestrian crossings. Also, we should slow down when making turns. A good driver accelerates smoothly and does not change lanes erratically.

By avoiding sudden and hard stops, a car can be better maintained and its life extended. A cabdriver can drive a car for ten years, whereas others will wear it out in five. The reason is most people step hard on the brakes when they approach stoplights, but a cabdriver knows to slow down from afar and gently step on the brakes while approaching the stoplight

The power of cars is not to be underestimated! The United States once conquered Japan with its weapons, but the Japanese have overtaken America with their cars. The automobile industry is very profitable and plays an important role in a country's economy.

BAGS

It is fashionable these days for people to carry a bag with them wherever they go. The bags can be of different sizes and materials, such as plastic, paper, leather, or cloth. However, bags used to be flat. It was not until recently that our bags, regardless of size, have begun to bulge.

Now we have bags for men and women at work or play. We can even discern one's social status or income from looking at his or her bag. This is especially the case with men's bags, which are good indicators of affluence in people's lifestyles and society.

Through the ages, people's choice of bags have been closely related to the events of their times. During the Japanese occupation of China, people carried bags made of nets. By putting the contents of their bags in plain view to reduce or avoid any trouble, they could pass through the various checkpoints quickly.

Bags are a lifelong accessory that no one can live without. During elementary school, we carry schoolbags full of books, candies, toys, and sometimes even our pets. When we are young adults, we need bags that accommodate our files, business cards, credit cards, money, cell phones, and address books. Young women keep cosmetics in their bags for touching up their make-up. This shows that their nature is to pursue beauty. A married woman with a young child, on the other hand, carries bottles, diapers, and baby wipes in her bag, a sign that she cares more about her baby than her face. By the time we are old, medication probably replaces everything else as the most important item.

Even animals have pouches, such as koala bears and kangaroos. In reality, the human mind is very much like a bag, which can hold everything and anything. While some people's minds are superficial and full of junk, others are substantive and deeply thoughtful. If we are broad-minded in our understanding, we embrace the universe in our minds. However, if we are narrow-minded in our views, we will not be able to hold anything within, not even a word, a small deed, or a person. Everything becomes a burden that is too heavy to bear.

Our bags need not be designer brands to be practical, appro-

priate, or useful. The best bag that we can have is within ourselves. If we can keep loving-kindness, compassion, wisdom,
right views, right understanding, and good and meritorious deeds
in our minds, we will have everything we need for daily life.

PENS

The inventions of paper and pen have contributed immensely to civilization. Since the beginning of time, there have been different kinds of pens, in the form of brushes, pencils, quills, ballpoint, rollerball pens, etc. In the past, people used willow twigs, reeds, and even their fingers as pens. Many western painters employed a variety of methods and objects instead of a brush in their artistic creations. Loyal ministers and devout children often left behind scripts and stories of sorrow and heroism, written with blood from their fingers.

People have praised historians for the just way they have recorded history. Famed Chinese scholar Liang Qichao was not moved by a bribe offered to him by the traitor of his time, and used his pen to overthrow the illegitimate regime. So the question is-which is more powerful: guns or pens? While guns and mortar can kill and wound, the fatalities and injuries are limited. The effect of people's writings is deep and wide. Therefore, in the past, scholars and generals prevailed by using their brushes or pens to save their country and citizens.

When we save someone from the gun or sword, it is only for the moment, but when we save someone with a pen it lasts for ages. Since the beginning of time, the pen of a judge has represented justice, and the pen of scholars and poets has contributed to a country's rich culture. Chinese calligraphers have left many pieces of artwork with their brushes. Some renowned examples are Venerable Master Huaisu's *Diamond Sutra* and Wang Xizhi's preface to the Lan Ting Collection. Young people today still learn the four classic kinds of Chinese calligraphy.

The Nationalist Party of China relied on the righteous spirit of national heroes to overthrow the Qing Dynasty. The Communist Party, on the other hand, depended on the pens of many literary types of the time to change the minds of the people and establish a new regime. So even though the Nationalists were equipped with strong military power, they could not overcome the pens of writers.

Today, with the invention of new technology, the indomitable

power of the pen is being replaced with the computer. Since people can type much faster on a computer and computer print is neater than handwriting, we change with the times. As we remember the contributions of the pen to civilization, we also hope that the different kinds of pens in the world can continue to create glory for people and nations.

BAGGAGE

How heavy is the baggage of life? Besides the physical bags and luggage that we carry around with us everywhere, we shoulder many other types of mental, cultural, and sentimental baggage. Life is full of trials and tribulations, forcing us to haul our baggage around from our youth to old age.

When others treat us well in our relationships, they become baggage for us in terms of emotions and sentiments. If they are unkind, we are burdened with negative feelings and rejection. In our families, basic groceries and utilities are economic baggage. The right and wrong between self and others, as well as the benevolence and badness of people, can easily become the baggage of our constant ethical battles. Greed, anger, ignorance, and worries are often the baggage of our spirit.

In addition to the unavoidable burden of making a living, people frequently carry cultural baggage with them. For instance, when building a new home, some people want to verify the "feng shui" of the site, or when opening a new business, they seek the best hour to do so. They are all adding unnecessary weight to their burden. Some people create an extra mental load for themselves because of a few stray words or a gesture someone makes. There are already so many burdens in life that we have to deal with: our health and physical body, our responsibility to family, our contributions to society, and love for our country. Life is certainly tough, so how can we live in ease while we carry around so many burdens of the world?

While "having" is baggage, so is "not having." The same goes for good and bad. However, people enjoy carrying some burdens around, because though there are troubles in every load, there is also joy and laughter. For instance, children are sweet burdens for parents to shoulder. When people help others solve problems, there are always some less pleasant burdens attached.

Buddhism teaches us how to deal with baggage. When we need to use it, we pick it up, and when we do not need it anymore, we just put it down. We should learn to pick up things when appropriate, and let them go as necessary. On the other hand, if we

do not pick things up when we should, we fail to use them properly. When we continue to carry a load instead of letting go and living in ease, we feel burdened.

We can look to Monk Budai's philosophy to help guide our conduct and handle our affairs. He could "carry all in his big belly, carrying everything there is in the world." He told us to "laugh all the time; laugh away all the sorrow since the beginning of time!" He often said, "What ease there is in putting down the bag we have carried while walking and sitting!" If we let go of the baggage of all the big and small burdens in life, we can truly live in ease and peace!

KALEIDOSCOPE

In the past, especially in farming regions and villages, children could not afford to buy toys, so they used cardboard paper and mirrors to create kaleidoscopes. These makeshift toys helped provide many people a beautiful childhood.

Kaleidoscopes make use of optics. A tube is formed with three pieces of long narrow mirror and is wrapped with hard paper. The center contains some colorful confetti. One end is sealed with glass and an opening is cut into the other end so that as the tube is turned, endless colors and changes can be seen through the opening. So children find them very interesting and fun to play with.

Life in today's society is a kaleidoscope. There are different kinds of people. They may be wise, foolish, rich, poor, noble, lowly, tall, short, fat, thin, young, old, male or female, all with different faces. There are all sorts of issues: major, minor, good, bad, domestic, and national. The community has various organizations, activities, schools, languages, shops, products, and so forth. When we look at life closely, it is as colorful and dazzling as a kaleidoscope.

The world is indeed a diverse place for beings of the five realms, because life is filled with truth, falsehood, good, bad, wise, foolish, Buddha, and the devil. Like a kaleidoscope, it is not easy to tell the difference between all these. When we look up at the sky while standing under the hot sun, we feel dizzy. When we reach beyond the kaleidoscope, we will be able to see life and society more clearly.

In reality, life in a kaleidoscope is nothing but the pursuit of fame and fortune. Some people do not even have the drive to pursue fame and fortune. They live a mixed-up life everyday. They are like pigs, horses, cows and sheep, that have nothing else to look forward to but food and water.

Other people cultivate themselves and feel that they have already transcended the Three Realms, so they think they no longer reside within this world. Such a life is like looking at flowers in the fog and not seeing any of them clearly. When we are

able to view society objectively and appreciate life for what it is, we will be able to see things differently.

Some people look at the ever-changing and complicated kaleidoscopic world with a magnifying glass, a microscope, a telescope, or even x-rays. But is it possible to see this colorful world clearly, even when we use a triple magnifying glass?

We are often mesmerized by the kaleidoscope of life because of our inadequate wisdom and insufficient powers of observation. We simply go with the flow, and fail to see its true face. Therefore, the Buddha asked us to look at the mind. We should not follow the colorful changes of a kaleidoscope. Rather, we should follow our true heart and self-nature by living a truthful life. When we return to the original self, we gain truth and find our true life.

A PIECE OF PAPER

Why were we born into this world? For a piece of paper!
After our mothers give birth to us, the hospital issues a birth certificate. Then we must be properly registered with the appropriate
government agency. Growing up, we receive certificates for
schooling in kindergarten, primary and high schools, as well as
college. All of these are pieces of paper.

When couples marry, they receive a marriage certificate,
which allows them to remain legally married. If they no longer
love one another and decide to separate, their divorce is also ver-
ified by a piece of paper from the authorities. Sadder still, when
we die the verification of death is nothing but a piece of paper.

A piece of paper has major functions. We are rewarded for
hard work and achievements with a letter of commendation. In the
courts, the verdict is written on paper. Traffic tickets and tax
penalties are pieces of paper that we have to deal with. We rejoice
or get upset over a piece of paper, because it brings us either good
or bad news.

Every profession or specialized skill we study and learn
requires certification in the form of a piece of paper. For instance,
doctors and lawyers need licenses to practice their professions, as
do chefs, beauticians, hairdressers, and bartenders. And we all
need a driver's license to drive. It is easier to get a job with proper skill certifications, which represent proof of our professionalism. If we do not have anything to show others what we do best,
the doors to employment are difficult to open.

Some people own extensive property, the titles and deeds to
which are recorded on pieces of paper. In many cases, a person's
financial wealth can be measured according to the number of such
pieces of paper that he or she possesses.

In maintaining mutual trust among people, we sometimes
need a contract as a safeguard. When it comes to diplomacy
between countries, all equal or unequal treaties are in writing. In
everyday life, the average worker counts out how much money he
or she earns, while wealthier people may use checks on a regular
basis.

When we are the guarantor for someone, we often have to co-sign contracts and certificates, consequently taking up legal obligations. While it is just a piece of paper that we write on, the results can be serious because we may lose everything we have if the other party defaults.

When we travel outside the country, we first have to apply for a passport. In addition, we need a visa to enter the country we are visiting, which can be difficult to obtain at times. There are of course issues in life that are not easy to understand, but sometimes a simple piece of paper is enough to send us running around in circles. Therefore, in modern life, the function and power of a mere piece of paper should never be underestimated!

SIGNS AND MILESTONES

Along roads and streets, there are many signs and milestones to provide guidelines about speed limits, directions, passing, turning, etc. In public places, signs direct people to elevators, emergency exits, restrooms, and public telephones. The signs indicate the correct direction, so that people can follow them where they need to go.

Some people are not accustomed to using their eyes to read signs but instead prefer to use their mouths to ask others for direction. Even when someone explains something to them, they do not pay attention and afterwards wander everywhere asking other people. We often see members of tour groups who never listen when their guide is talking to them, and afterwards immediately start asking where the restaurant or restroom is.

The road of life has many signs and milestones as well. There are economic, relationship, and life planning signs and milestones. In addition, a country must develop itself according to certain signs and milestones with respect to diplomacy, defense, education, and even five-year and ten-year plans.

As for the milestones of life, if we only support ourselves, we only focus on one individual. If the milestone is to maintain a family, we can become the head of household. However, if the milestone is to serve people, then we can become a leader.

There are also milestones in our careers. For instance, if you study literature, the milestone of your life is to become a literary person. If you study medicine, the milestone of your life is to become a doctor. If you study business, then your milestone is to become a businessperson. If you study technology, you strive to become a technician. If you study finance and economics or law and politics, then these are the milestones of your life.

Therefore, we must set milestones in life. The bigger the goals, the greater the achievements. Even if the milestone is far removed, as long as you work hard, you will achieve it. The journey of life may be long, but if we take it one step at a time, surely and steadily, how can we not reach our milestones?

Today, the milestones for some people are to make money and gain a high position. Many people play the lotto; their milestone is money. When millions of people bet their money on a regular basis, how many of their milestones point to ethics and morals? Other people set their sights on high positions and public office. There are seemingly constant elections for mayors, legislators, senators, congressmen, and even for president. The goal is fame. However, when these people reach their milestones, they often lose sight of ethics and morals, which is most regrettable!

We should all have milestones based on ethics and morals. Confucianism's "Three Bonds and Five Constant Virtues" guides human relations, and Buddhism's "Four Embracing Virtues and Six Perfections" guide us in cultivation through helping others; we should follow the direction of both of these "signs" to achieve milestones in human relations and cultivation in our lives.

TO RELIEVE ALL SUFFERING

Life is a glass of bitter wine, full of suffering. At birth, our first cry indicates suffering. Afterwards, we face ups and downs and all sorts of difficulties on the journey of life. Tasting all its bitterness, we all want to be free from pain and suffering and live in happiness. But where is happiness?

We look for happiness in many different ways and places. We turn to religion for happiness. We unite with others, forming political parties and trade unions to improve our sense of security. We save for a rainy day by buying property and depositing money in the bank. We have children in the hope that they will take care of us when we grow old. We pursue knowledge or try to raise our social status. We all wish to exchange our suffering for happiness. In the search for happiness, we cannot escape suffering. As the saying goes, "Men die for money." Even if we gain fame and fortune, we still suffer the pain of birth, aging, sickness, and death. We have to face sadness, joy, separations, and gatherings. How do we get relief from all the suffering?

Many people believe that suffering means the lack of something, such as money, fame, power, or status. Real suffering, however, comes from having these things. For instance, when we have a family, love and a career, the suffering from "having" these is countless. The *Heart Sutra* states, "By contemplating the emptiness of the five components of existence, all suffering is relieved." Suffering comes from the "self" that is created by the combination of the five components of existence: physical form, perception, conception, mental formation, and consciousness. For example, some suffering arises from the failure to obtain what the self wants. Some suffering is a result of incompatibility between the self and the environment. Some suffering is due to the discord between self and others, where enemies meet and love departs. Other suffering comes from man-made and natural disasters.

Greed, hate, wrong views, sadness, and worries that exist in the self and the mind make suffering all the more intolerable. Since life's suffering comes from the "self," in order to relieve all suffering, we must empty the self and release all attachments. We

must be able to contemplate the emptiness of the five components of existence, actualize our wisdom, understand the closeness between self and others, and harmonize self and phenomena. Then we will be able to simplify and resolve the relationship between "self" and phenomena, the environment, other people, society, nature, and even the body and mind. Only when we can live peacefully and freely, without attachments and defilement, can we truly relieve all suffering.

WALKING, STANDING, SITTING AND RESTING

Buddhist Etiquette says, "Walk like the wind, stand like a pine, sit like a bell, and rest like a bow." This basic etiquette not only applies to Buddhists; everyone should practice it in daily living.

When we first meet a person, we can tell the level of the person's education and cultivation by his or her manners. We know how refined a person is by his or her speech and conduct.

When a country sends diplomats to foreign countries as ambassadors, it needs to train them first in diplomatic etiquette, especially in the manner in which they conduct themselves, so that their home country will be well-represented.

In the family, parents educate their children to be polite and to cultivate good habits in life. The basic manners of walking, standing, sitting and resting are the first important lessons for everyone. In school, teachers should not only convey knowledge to their students; life skills education and fundamental acceptable behaviors are just as important.

However, in today's society we often see that only debutantes and flight attendants are trained in etiquette. Today's young people have many learning problems because of the lack of emphasis on life education. They walk, stand, sit, and rest in poor form. They do not conduct themselves properly. Many people keep pets. Good pets do not run wild or sleep anywhere they want to; they are well trained and listen to the orders of their owners. As humans, supreme among all living beings, how can we not have good manners?

In reality, how we walk, stand, sit, and rest is not restricted to outward expression. When parrots talk and monkeys behave like people, they are still not human. Good manners emanate from within and are reflected in our behavior. Refined walking, standing, sitting, and resting start within the mind and look as if they are second nature.

Therefore, those who have not cultivated good manners as a part of their habits will end up embarrassing themselves and those

around them. In Chan Buddhism there are lessons to be learned, even in a glance or facial expression. There is Dharma in eating and sleeping. Every activity and body movement a Buddhist practitioner makes while walking, standing, sitting and sleeping is in accord with Buddhism due to long periods of cultivation.

The renowned Chinese philosopher Cheng Yi once saw monastics in a Buddhist temple lining up for their meditative meal and exclaimed, "The essence of the etiquette of the generations is here!" Thus, for those who know Humanistic Buddhism well, the beauty and fragrance of cultivation lies in walking, standing, sitting, and resting.

TEAMWORK

As the saying goes, "A single tree does not make a forest." To make a car drivable, people first need to assemble the engine, tires, seats, dashboard, and other parts. A building needs engineers, architects, and workers from different trades to work together to plan and construct it. Editors, reporters, distributors, and printers collaborate to publish a newspaper. A television program needs producers, directors, writers, and actors to be produced. Different governmental departments, such as state and foreign affairs, finance, education, and defense coordinate efforts so that governments can function and develop.

The human body is the result of teamwork. A human needs different body parts and systems to work together to be healthy: the nose and mouth to breathe, the digestive system to digest food, and the heart to pump blood throughout the body. In addition, the hands have to move, the legs need to walk, and the six sense organs of eye, ear, nose, tongue, body, and mind must cooperate in order for the body to function properly.

Teamwork does not only apply to human beings. Even flowers and plants need the nourishment of wind, rain, and sunshine. The four elements of heat, earth, air, and water must be combined to make bricks or tiles.

Teamwork is conditional origination. If there are no conditions, then nothing can be accomplished. If there is no teamwork, it is like a machine with a screw missing. No matter how wonderful the machine is, it is still useless. In a team, no one person is more important than another. Everyone is important in his or her own way. In competing for importance, we should not judge how big or small a person's contribution is. For example, look at the face. Each feature is vital; even the seemingly useless eyebrows enhance the appearance of the whole face. For successful teamwork, we need to respect each other and praise others for their contributions. We should not dwell on our own successes.

In a basketball game, if one player tries to carry the game by himself, the team will surely lose. It takes the cooperation of the center and the guards to win the game. In badminton, even though

just two players compete, the game cannot be played without the coaches and referees, and all the other people who provide the equipment and space. Cement, sand, and rocks must be mixed well to form concrete. The fingers and thumb need to join together to form a fist before they can hit forcefully.

In teamwork, "me" is only a member and not the whole, because everything is actually causes and conditions. The team shares common goals and efforts, not just the person. Teamwork is the truth, which does not spell one. In other words, one is all and all is one. They complement each other.

Today, society emphasizes teamwork because personal achievements are often limited. When we pull together the wisdom of many, we can create better results. Therefore, in our interactions with others at work, we need to respect and tolerate one another. We should make "getting the job done well" our top priority.

In writing history, sometimes we need to write about our personal achievements as a means of encouragement. However, we should also promote writing the history of team creations that result from the concentration of efforts and the communication of views. Superiors need the support of their subordinates, and vice versa. True teamwork can be accomplished and the glory of success shared when we complement one another.

KEEPING A DISTANCE

Sometimes we see signs on the highway that warn us to keep a safe distance from other cars. However, truthfully, everything and everyone must learn to keep a safe distance, and not only while we are driving.

The human body is one example. Our eyes, nose, and mouth are all located away from one another. Our internal organs have their positions. Our teeth and tongue must keep a distance, because it hurts when we accidentally bite our own tongue.

When we plant trees, vegetables and flowers, we must measure the right distance between them so they can grow well. The distance between the words and sentences in an article should be right, to allow easy reading.

When communities build apartment complexes, there is often too little space in between and as a result much conflict takes place among the neighbors. If there is more space for fences and walls, keeping a distance between them, then even children may not fight as much.

When we view a painting, we need to see it from a certain distance to truly appreciate its beauty. When reading a book or newspaper, our eyes will see clearly and not hurt when we do so from the right distance. We keep our homes a safe distance from water sources, so that the water will not be contaminated. We need to keep a safe distance from criminals and other undesirable elements.

Some people fail to keep a distance from harmful matters in exchange for profits. They find it difficult to stay away from these things. For instance, some people use drugs because they are curious or for health reasons, and eventually they become addicted. They find it difficult to give up their addiction. Keeping a distance from drugs, when necessary, is very important.

On highways and roads, there are medians, double yellow lines, bypass areas, and similar installations. They are all built to keep distance between moving vehicles for safe driving. In hospitals, quarantine areas are designated with warning signs so that people keep away. In zoos, signs warn people to keep a safe dis-

tance from wild, caged animals to avoid possible attack and unnecessary injuries. In the park, certain regions are kept off limits to protect the plants and flowers growing there. We also keep a distance from high voltage wires, and polluted air, steep cliffs, and rushing rivers.

Additionally, we must keep unwholesome thoughts, ideas, and actions and speech that may hurt others at a distance. But, while we should keep a distance from everyone and everything that is bad and dangerous, we should remain close to that which is good and benevolent.

A LOW PROFILE

When elders of great virtue give us advice on how to conduct ourselves, they always say keep a "low profile."

Keeping a low profile means showing humility, respect, friendly gestures, and courtesy. However, a low profile is not easily cultivated and takes years of practice to achieve. By cultivating a low profile, it makes it easier for us to deal with other people and different types of situations.

Keeping a low profile does not mean simply kowtowing all the time. When we need to take a stand on moral grounds, we must stand tall and hold our heads high because it is important to do so. Yen Ying of the Epoch of Spring and Autumn was not even five feet tall. Because he treated everyone with humility, he appeared even shorter. Once he was on a mission in the Qin Kingdom and the officials there only opened a small door to receive him. Yen refused to enter and said, "I learned that when on a mission to a large kingdom, I walk through a large door and only use a small door when visiting a dog kingdom. The Qin Kingdom is large; how can I walk through a dog door?" Qin officials had no choice but to open the large door for him.

Everything mature in this world always has a low profile. For instance, when rice is ripe and fully-grown, it always droops and hangs low. Weeping willows are gentle and droop low, so even when the wind and rain blow hard on them, they do not break. This illustrates that in any matter or with any person, if we are flexible and resilient and keep a low profile, we will benefit.

Countries like Switzerland and Sweden are neutral, so they do not engage in war. By keeping a low profile in the world and avoiding fighting, not only are they known as countries of peace, but they also have international reputations as good as that of large countries.

As the sayings go, "A full bottle makes no noise, while a half-empty bottle makes more noise," and "Oceans are quiet, while brooks gurgle." Those who are not truly learned or cultivated always make their presence felt and their voices heard as they strut about in arrogance. On the other hand, the truly learned

always keep a low profile everywhere they go. Others can appreciate their morals, cultivation, and greatness in their low profile.

Someone once wanted to build a house that was only five feet high. The architect explained, "It is not easy to build a house five feet high, and nobody wants one anyway." The person replied, "I am the one who wants it built." The architect again said, "It is impossible to enter or stand up in a five foot high house." The person answered, "If I keep a low profile, I can save a lot on building costs. Why are you worried about me?"

In a race, cyclists all stoop as low as possible, because a low profile will reduce resistance. Runners start off a race by stooping down, waiting for the signal to charge ahead. As the saying goes, "High trees attract the wind, but drooping branches remain tough." People may hold their heads high or low in life and speak in a loud or soft voice. We usually prefer people who are soft spoken and keep a low profile, and want to make connections with them. They are like gentle spring breezes, putting others at ease, and making it easy for people to like and be close to them.

OUR ORIGINAL FACE

People can mask their faces, but facades cannot withstand the test of time, because only a person's original or true face can go through time unchanged. The wise, the mean, the loyal, and the treacherous all have a true face. When actors make an entrance on stage, their makeup informs the audience immediately whether they are playing good or evil roles.

In some places, there is a law that when people go to church they should not put on makeup or wigs, in order to meet god with a true face. Buddhists cultivate in order to know their own true face. There is a verse, "If people can recognize their true faces as given by their mother (prajna-wisdom, mother of Buddhas), life and the world will be filled with light." Chan masters spend decades contemplating the saying, "What was my true faces before my parents gave birth to me?" and are often unsatisfied with the answer.

However, many people in the world are easily misunderstood, and their true faces are distorted. Support, slander, criticism, and jealousy can easily mask people's true faces. It is difficult enough to see our own face, let alone that of others.

In the Chinese classic novel, *Journey to the West*, Venerable Xuanzhuang is a caricature of a cowardly person who retreats in the face of difficulties. In reality, he was the pride and glory of the Chinese people. In his journey to the West, he passed through long miles of quicksand, and as he trekked across mountains and water he met hardships of all kinds. He displayed tremendous courage, perseverance, and a strong spirit in his mission, and was the first ambassador of Chinese culture in a foreign land. His Tang Journal of the Western Region enabled the eight major Buddhist holy sites in India that had been destroyed by invading Muslims and Hindus to be revived later in history. The true face of such a legendary master of the time was, however, distorted by the novel. So today people are re-editing Xuanzhuang's Western Journey in the hope of rebuilding his image.

In reality, everything in nature has a true face. Environmentalists believe that green is the true face of the earth,

and clear water that of brooks and rivers. Social workers think that love, harmony, community, and morality are the true face of society. Those advocating humanistic education consider an individual's honesty, compassion, and peacefulness as the true face of the world.

Chan Master Lingyun Zhiqin said, "After searching for three decades, as leaves fall and branches grow on trees, once one sees the true face, there is no doubt anymore." The great scholar Su Dongpo wrote, "We fail to know the true face of Mount Lu because we are inside the mountain." If we can find our true heart, that is our true face.

HOSPITALITY

Once a Westerner visited Taiwan and made a very fair comment. He said, "Chinese people are very hospitable but lack public mindfulness." This is so true! Chinese people place much emphasis on hospitality and believe "the more polite, the better." But they have less regard for social order and public morals.

Since olden times, Chinese hospitality has been shown in various ways, from free roadside tea to nightlights provided for travelers. When friends visit, if there are no extra accommodations available, the hosts give up their own beds and use the couch or floor in the living room. They will do anything to accommodate friends for the night. When sharing a meal with friends and relatives, they heap food on their guests' plates and make sure they have as much to eat as possible. Even if their budget is tight, hosts will borrow from another person or pawn their possessions in order to treat a friend to dinner. These all show the hospitality of the Chinese.

Today, when the Chinese provide relief during emergencies and disasters or when they console the sick and injured, especially lonely senior citizens, they not only go themselves but also ensure that their neighbors and the community get involved as well. It appears that there are good people everywhere in society. However, some people pocket relief funds and make a living by taking advantage of the old and sick. This is immoral.

When we visit others, we should always bring a gift, and if someone comes to our home, we should give them something to show our hospitality. In Taiwan, a gift is also called a "hand companion" because when someone from the family travels, he or she needs to bring something home for other members, especially children. Even neighbors can share in the gift as well. Such is Chinese hospitality!

People in the old days left rice out for mice and refrained from lighting lamps for the sake of moths and bugs that fly around and might get burnt by the fire. They would rather grope around in the dark than fail to be hospitable to animals. While keeping pets is a habit for Westerners, Chinese kept dogs and cats even

when they could not really afford to do so. They were not really keeping pets as such but felt that they should be friends with animals. Some homemakers did not travel for years because their children were too young to bring along, or there were cats and dogs they had to care for. Sometimes neighbors lent a helping hand and volunteered to look after the animals while their owners were away.

It is common practice to housesit for our neighbors, help in one another's fields during harvest, bring the whole family over to lend a hand for special occasions, such as weddings or funerals, and congratulate and render support when people we know open a new store. When a young couple marries or a senior citizen celebrates a birthday, these are special times to express our friendliness.

All of these are examples of Chinese hospitality. However, although it is good to praise such hospitality, our real hope in doing so is to foster greater social consciousness everywhere and make all of our communities more complete.

BRAKING

There are many lessons to learn in life; knowing when to step on the brakes is a very important one. The causes of many mishaps or misfortunes are the result of poor "braking." For instance, when talking to another person, we should stop if the conversation is not going well. When making a public speech, if we fail to conclude when we should and ramble on with "another point," "one more thing" or "furthermore," our audience will find us tedious.

When workers in an organization spread gossip or opinions about certain changes, the manager or supervisor should step on the brakes and take a good look at what is going on. Similarly, politicians should know it is time to stop and review the situation if their policies are creating dissatisfaction among the public.

Those who are learning to drive, whether it is a car, boat or plane, must know how to work the brakes. This is especially so with flying; as the plane descends on the runway, it is very important to control the speed so the plane does not slide off or come to an abrupt halt. If passengers on the plane feel erratic stops when braking, the pilot is not doing a good job.

A couple that lives together may fight every now and then. As long as the fights are not hurtful, they are harmless. However, some fights may escalate into a "cold war," repulsion, suspicion, and even accusations of extramarital affairs. Whether there are actual betrayals or not, knowing how to step on the brakes is crucial for a happy ending. If the fighting persists and neither knows when to stop, then no matter how deep their love is for one another, the marriage will likely end in divorce.

When people make friends, they may get along so well that it is unbearable to be apart from one another. Then it may be wise to cool things off. Some friends may disagree with or be angry at each other. This may also be a good time to cool things off. If there are people in our circle of friends who take up unwholesome habits, such as drugs, gambling or drinking, we should help them stop before it gets out of control. Otherwise, the consequences can be dire.

People who operate their own businesses or make their own investments should know when to step on the brakes if they lose money often or are investing too much capital. Since the bottomless pit of endless greed can never be filled, not knowing when to stop is very dangerous. We often see people play the stock market or even the lotto. They should exercise caution in the amount they invest because safeguarding their bottom line is very important. It is like vehicles on the highways; most of the accidents are the result of speeding motorists who fail to brake in time.

In the course of their practice, religious practitioners may have regrets or become disheartened. They, too, should step on the brakes and stop their digressions. Many people today tend to overwork. If they fail to brake, they may even die from fatigue, which is certainly not worth it. Quitting while we are ahead and braking appropriately reflects wisdom in life that we cannot do without.

SOUL

To exist, we need a physical body and mental power or inner spirit. The mental component of our existence is commonly called a "soul." What is a soul? It is something vital to a person's survival that distinguishes the living from the non-living.

When someone appears listless, we say that he or she lacks energy. When someone's life is in disarray, we ask if he or she has lost his or her spirit. Therefore, it is clear that a person's wellness depends on the soundness of his or her soul.

It is important for an organization to have a person who can be its "heart and soul." It is imperative for a country to have a leader who is full of vigor and vitality. The soul is the foundation of human activity. With it, the human body will function properly.

The belief that the soul only exists after death is a myth, for the soul is the force that gives light to a person's eyes, extra bounce to a person's step, and inspires a person with courage, confidence, and intelligence. It is the energy behind a person's demeanor and appearance.

Since the soul is the source of life and vitality, it enables us to be nimble with our work, quick-witted in our speech, ingenious in our ways, spiritual with our thoughts, and inspirational with our words. Some people have even described a couple's love as two hearts beating as one and sharing the same soul.

Although the soul has been thoroughly researched in both the eastern and western worlds, it is not a topic of discussion in Buddhism, which focuses on the mind and its functions, not the soul. Generally speaking, the soul can only reach the sixth consciousness, which is associated with normal mental activities. If we have an understanding of the sixth consciousness, we can achieve a state of ordinary intelligence; but there exists an eighth consciousness, the conditioned subject of transmigration. This is truly the most important part of life.

If we want to have insight into the eighth consciousness, we must possess the wisdom of the highest enlightenment, because knowledge alone is not enough. How can we realize the state of

perfect wisdom? We must rely on cultivation and realization. If we can transform the eighth consciousness into the "four forms of wisdom"-the first five consciousness's "perfecting wisdom," the sixth consciousness's "profound observing wisdom," the seventh consciousness's "impartial wisdom," and the eighth consciousness's "great mirror wisdom"-then we will not only have a soul, but also the presence of Buddha Nature. When our Buddha Nature is thus manifested, life will be complete, without attachment, defilement, and hindrance.

"The soul is immortal and the spirit never dies" has been used to describe life after death. Although it is a reasonable statement, it is not the ultimate truth. Our true nature lies in nirvana, the state of tranquility and purity, where the mind is detached and non-clinging. Accordingly, "Through great wisdom, there is no abiding in birth and death; through great compassion, there is no abiding in nirvana." This is our true nature.

FORTUNE TELLING

During the Yuan Dynasty, there was a self-proclaimed fortuneteller who was not shy about claiming the ability to foretell the future. One day, he came across three students who were on their way to a very important examination. Worried about their future, the young men asked the fortuneteller to predict the outcome of the test. After a few seconds, the fortuneteller held out one finger and said, "You will know when the time is right, for I cannot reveal the heavenly secret." After the students left, the fortuneteller's assistant asked him curiously, "Who will actually pass the test?" He replied, "It is very easy to understand the reasoning behind my gesture. If one of them passes the test, the one finger will be correct in foretelling the future. If two of them pass the test, the one finger will be right in saying that one of them failed the test. If they all pass or fail the test, the one finger will be accurate in its prediction that all three share the same fate. Therefore, we have all the answers in one finger."

What is our destiny, if we do have one? Our destiny is the karmic retribution that is born out of our words, deeds, and thoughts. So, we do indeed have a destiny. However, whatever our destiny may be, it is certainly not predetermined. We are the architects of our own destiny, which can be changed by a word, a person, an event, an idea, or a single dollar. A young novice monk had only seven days to live, but because he had saved a colony of ants, his seven days turned into a long life of eighty years. Therefore, destiny is not predetermined; we can change the course of destiny with good and meritorious deeds.

We do not need a fortuneteller to tell our fortune. We can do it ourselves. As the saying goes, "If we want to know our past life, we need not look any further than our present life. If we want to know our future life, all we need to do is look at our present life." Isn't it clear, then, that the past, present, and future are all-inclusive as causes and conditions? Therefore, if we want to change our destiny, we must first change our behaviors and habits, since our temperament is determined by our habits, which in turn are the bases of our actions, and thus change our destiny.

It is easy for us to see our destiny, since it is either written on our faces or manifested through our words and deeds. Even our rapid thought process is crucial to our destiny. A good thought means ascending to the realm of celestial beings, and a bad thought leads us to the realm of neverending hell. Since our minds never stop working, 24 hours a day, 365 days a year, our good and bad thoughts are constantly at play in determining our destiny.

Once upon a time, there was a fortuneteller famous for making accurate predictions. One day a man visited him in the hope of learning his future. After the fortuneteller had carefully studied his horoscope, the man got up and left without saying a word. Bewildered, the fortuneteller chased him and asked why he had left so abruptly. "Since you are so good at foretelling other's fortunes, can't you tell in advance that I am not only broke but also penniless?" Therefore, it is imperative for us to understand that we are in control of our own destiny, and that our fortunes are made inside our minds.

EACH HAS ITS OWN PARENTS

The Conference of Multi-faith Leaders held at the Roman Catholic Archdiocese Office was attended by representatives from ten major religions. Since it was a rare occasion for people from so many religions to gather in one place, as a friendly gesture and acknowledgement of the fundamental spirit of religion, someone advocated that the icons of all the religions be honored at the same time. Many of the representatives supported the suggestion, but Archbishop Lou Guang indicated that if this happened, he would not be able to worship.

Although the followers of various religions can mingle, their teachings are different and consequently their religious icons should not be assembled in one place. We should understand clearly that your parents are not my parents, and religious icons are like parents. How can we possibly mix them?

Differences as well as similarities always exist among religions. Within the similarities we can seek common ground. A frequent claim is, "Religions all teach people to do good." We should not, however, insist that they all be the same. Different religions have their own practices and levels of understanding. It is like the functions of our limbs. Why do arms need to be legs, or vice versa? Basically, we should tolerate the existence of all religions in order to achieve beauty, trueness, and goodness in life.

By respecting the existence of religious differences, we should also recognize similarities in religions, human beings, compassion, and the pursuit of benevolence. Followers should, therefore, be supportive, friendly, and respectful of each other. But there is no need for them to take each other's parents as their own.

People today tend to be dualistic about everything. Something is good or bad, yours or mine, true or false, likeable or unlikeable. They only succeed in being divisive instead of unifying. Rather, we should be clear that although our parents are different we can still be classmates or friends.

Buddhism teaches, "There are many skillful means but only one path to the truth." The religions of the world should contemplate this teaching.

THE ABHORRENCE OF DELUSION

What is the most fearful condition in this world? Poverty, hunger, thirst, terror, hopelessness¡K these are all fearful, but in reality delusion is the most fearful. Being deluded means the lack of reasoning. Those who cannot reason hold distorted and deviant views. Their unwholesome thoughts and actions not only affect themselves adversely but also influence others for generations to come.

The Buddha could not emphasize enough the importance of wisdom. He told many stories of delusion and folly to illustrate its harm. Similarly, there are many Chinese fables that describe the results of delusion. Throughout history, infamous criminals committed terrible crimes and ended up in jail. Other people betrayed their countries out of ignorance and greed for profit. Their acts of treason earned them notoriety and the hatred of their countrymen that lastes for generations. These are acts of delusion and its effects.

We see many examples of delusion in today's society. People who love to gamble believe that they can win in the end, and people who love to fight think they will never lose. Those who harm others only see how something benefits themselves, not the results of harming others. Strong-headed people are only concerned with venting their anger and not with the harm they do to their relationships. Investors play the market as day-traders in the pursuit of a quick buck; women buy far too many clothes and spend too much time cleaning them; wealthy people acquire too many properties and spend too many resources maintaining them. These are all acts of delusion.

People's failure to be realistic when faced with problems prevents them from finding the right solutions and getting to the core of the matter. This delusion is even worse than others. We often witness misguided government policies aimed at dealing with crucial issues such as global warming, power shortages, environmental protection, education, and health care, to name just a few. More often, the ends of such policies do not justify the means.

Delusion is much more serious than making mistakes.

Making mistakes is tripping and falling down while walking. One can always stand up again. Delusion is walking in the dark night with no lights to show the way. Delusion needs the light of wisdom to shine through. As the saying goes, "A dark room may exist for a thousand years; a light brightens it up right away. Delusion may last for eons; wisdom enlightens it instantly." If we can understand how awful delusion is, we will appreciate the importance of wisdom. Therefore, we need to develop the light of wisdom in our self-nature in order to create a bright future.

WHY WE ARE CHEATED

There are many ways to cheat people. We often hear about people being deceived by various types of scams, such as counterfeit products and money. The perpetrators may tell stories about their desperate need for cash, either playing on people's sympathy or greed to make a quick buck.

People are deceived because they do not think logically and fall for scams out of sympathy, but more often they are cheated because of their own greed! For example, a person may claim to have a valuable family heirloom, which he or she is willing to sell for half its value for some needed quick cash. If we were greedy for other's treasure, we would fall for this scam immediately. Another person may claim to own a piece of land that is worth millions and is willing to offer it as collateral for five hundred thousand dollars in cash. The person promises that once the land is sold, the loan and an additional hundred thousand in interest will be repaid right away. Unfortunately, after the loan is made, the duped lender discovers that the title to the land is counterfeit. There are countless incidents of scams. There are phone scams and many more on the Internet offering products and services that do not exist, which hapless consumers pay for with their credit cards. There are also so-called prizes for consumers to claim; they get fleeced when they call a toll number that puts them on hold for indefinite periods of time.

Fraud comes in many different forms. Even within a family, siblings swindle each other. In the workplace and among friends, people lie and cheat. Internationally, many people are involved in weapons, and economic and political scams.

However, deceiving ourselves is worse than being deceived by others. When we do not know our own intentions and thoughts or understand our causes and conditions, and put up a facade pretending to be what we are not, we deceive ourselves and the world. We may deceive our parents in exchange for what we want, deceive our lovers by exaggerating our qualities, deceive our co-workers, employers, and even ourselves by covering up shortcomings and mistakes. When we cheat each other, we are creating a world of mutual deceit and mistrust.

How do we free ourselves from deceit? The only way is to give up illusions and greed, and show our true face. By treating others with sincerity, we will be saved from deceit.

THE OUTFLOW OF MERIT

If we put the money we make in our pocket and it has a hole, the money will be lost. When we put things that we collect in a box or basket, the things will be lost if there are holes. Some people cultivate merit and make contributions. However, if they do not know how to guard their mind and thoughts and instead leave holes, their kind deeds will flow away in the same manner. This is really regrettable.

When some people make a donation, they are not completely willing to part with what they give and consequently hurt the self-respect of the recipient. The recipient will not only be ungrateful for the help but will also bear a grudge for the insult. Though the act of giving is benevolent, its merit will be lost. When we lend others a helping hand, if we inflate our self-importance they will act in opposition to us. Similarly, our merit will be lost.

Some people follow a certain faith and are influenced by its teachings to practice benevolence. They may have accumulated great merit exercising kindness in their speech, actions, and thoughts. However, if they meet with setbacks, they get upset and lose their temper. They become angry with themselves and blame everyone else for their misfortune. Any merit resulting from their kind deeds will be lost. We witness many people who have done kind deeds but do not enjoy the benefits. This is because there are too many holes in their karmas of body, speech, and thoughts. Their merits are lost naturally.

How do we prevent such outflows?

First, we mind our speech. Success and failure often hinge on a word. When we are humble and grateful, we add to our merit. However, if we hurt others with our words, our merit will be lost.

Second, we mind our actions. Since we already have done kind acts, we should nurture rather than ruin them. We should maintain them well, like the family car, and not abuse them.

Third, we mind our thoughts. In providing others with good causes and conditions, we should be positive. If we help others and regret it afterwards, our merit will be lost.

Some people throw their money away as they earn it, or trample on what they have planted. Like water leaking from a cracked glass or coins falling from a torn purse, no merit can be gained. The best merits in the world are often lost through our body, speech, and thoughts. Therefore, it is important for us to be mindful of our three karmas of body, speech and thoughts, so we do not lose our merits.

SEEING PROBLEMS CLEARLY

Once there was a group of blind men trying to "see" what an elephant looked like. Since they did not have eyesight, they used their hands instead. "It is like a hook," said the man who touched the elephant's trunk. "No, it is like a fan," said the one who touched the elephant's ears. "No, it is like a huge post," said the one who touched the elephant's legs. "No, it is like a drum," said the one who touched the elephant's belly. "No, you are all wrong; an elephant is like a broom," declared the one who touched the elephant's tail.

Although the blind men were able to partially describe the elephant, they were unable to come up with the complete picture. If we want to know what an elephant really looks like, we must use our wisdom eye. If we want to reach the heart of a problem, we must not make any assumptions beforehand. Therefore, to see a problem clearly is to look at it from all angles, inside and out. Once we have the full picture, we can fully grasp the heart of the matter.

There are many problems in this world involving family, friends, jobs, health, diet, financial situations, living arrangements, love, etc. Everyone has his or her own point of view. As a result, for every problem one has, many more are created. Since there are so many interpretations, different levels of acceptance, and various parties involved, a simple problem can be compounded and become something that is far more serious than it was initially.

While some people are good at creating problems, others are good at either seeing them clearly or solving them successfully. Problems are created when people are ignorant of causes and conditions. They are made when people fail to realize the nature and the degree of seriousness of any given situation. Because of their ignorance, they keep committing the same mistakes.

If a person can see a problem clearly, he or she will know the gist of it. However, if the person remains indifferent to the situation, playing it safe from afar, he or she will never be a problemsolver. On the other hand, a good problem-solver must have

favorable conditions on his or her side, as well as a good mind. He or she must be reasonable and understanding in knowing the ins and outs of a problem, so it can be solved with little or no trouble. Although some problems might be difficult to solve at first, a solution will eventually surface if we operate under the principle of bringing happiness to all parties concerned. We should never be deterred by obstacles. However, the biggest problem is not seeing a problem clearly. If we deal with people who are irrational and unreasonable, they will only make problems more complicated.

There is a story about a man who mistakenly put on shoes with different soles. As he walked out of his house, he felt very uncomfortable and said to himself, "What's wrong with my legs today? Why is one leg shorter than the other? Maybe the road is paved unevenly!" A passerby heard his comment and suggested to him, "You might be wearing two different shoes." The man then ordered his servant to hurry home and bring him the right shoes. After a while, the servant returned empty-handed and reported to his master, "It is not necessary to change your shoes because the shoes at home do not have matching soles either."

If we are unable to see a problem clearly, we will be as ignorant as the master and servant in the story. Therefore, it is imperative to cultivate our minds and develop our wisdom eye in order to see problems clearly.

MISTAKING THE MEANS FOR THE END

Everything has a natural origin and a sequence to arrive at its end. This is normal. However, if we mistake the means for the end, our actions and thinking can become muddled. There are many examples of things getting out of order or upside down. People invert levels of authority, confuse right and wrong, mix up priorities, and even reverse genders. This is not normal.

While many people advocate order and act rationally, quite a few are incapable of telling the difference between theory and practice, benefit and harm, trivial and important, or right and wrong. Like the saying, "trimming the feet to fit the shoes," there are numerous, unfocused people whose priorities are out of order.

Once a person bought a beautiful bookshelf but did not have any books to put in it. A curious friend asked why and was told that the man had sold all his books in order to buy the bookshelf. The Taipei Metro is affordable, efficient, and convenient for avoiding traffic jams. However, many people still drive and get stuck in traffic, all the while feeling helpless about being late for work.

Some people think eating in restaurants is worthwhile, even when there is food at home. Likewise, bakers do not appreciate their own products but instead enjoy bread from other bakeries. Some people ignore their parents while loving and honoring the parents of others, or treat their siblings like strangers while regarding their drinking buddies as their best friends.

The Buddha attained enlightenment while meditating on the diamond throne and watching the stars. Realizing how deluded sentient beings are, he wanted to enter nirvana immediately. He discovered that ignorance and attachments are the roots of delusion. However, sentient beings are best at holding onto delusion. While the Buddha believed that Dharma joy came from right faith and cultivation, sentient beings regard practice as suffering. The Buddha told us Buddha Nature is intrinsic and real, but sentient beings refuse to admit it. The Buddha perceived all phenomena as false and illusive, whereas sentient beings take them seriously and cling to them. This is why the Buddha said, "There are too many deluded sentient beings." Fortunately, Sakra, the heavenly king,

pleaded with the Buddha and he changed his mind.

Since the beginning of time, many saints and philosophers have preferred to argue with the wise rather than talk to those who mistake the means for the end. There are numerous people among us who spoil things with excessive enthusiasm; they carry the boat with them after they cross the river, or consider the finger pointed at the moon as the real target.

If we are not clear about order and principles, and confuse the end with the means, the results are often disastrous. Therefore, we should follow circumstances, understand both theory and practice, and know that all phenomena in the world are governed by cause and effect. If we follow the natural course of things, we will succeed as conditions ripen. Otherwise, when the sequence of things is out of order, we will suffer much loss in life.

DILEMMAS

We encounter many situations in life in which we are caught in a dilemma, not knowing how to choose. For instance, when parents fight, their children do not know whose side they should be on. When mother and daughter-in-law do not get along, which side should the son, who is also a husband, take? Once a man's mother and wife fell into the water at the same time. He did not know whom he should save first.

In Chinese history, many princesses were married off to a foreign state to salvage or establish diplomatic ties with the country. In their mission to harmonize the two states, these princesses often struggled between loyalty to their homeland and devotion to their husbands. During the Tang Dynasty, Princess Wencheng wed the ruler of Tibet. She endured many hardships while transmitting the culture and religion of her country to her adopted home, and her achievements were greatly admired. However, when she first left home for the distant state, news of her mother's terminal illness reached her. She became more homesick than ever and was stuck between her desire to go home to her parents and her duty to remain in her new home to continue her mission. It was a real dilemma!

During the Qing Dynasty, Princess Heshuo married the son of a Han royal family member in order to ease the relationship between the imperial court and the fiefdom. Before she left, the young and innocent princess asked her great grandmother, Queen Xiao Zhuang, "If one day the emperor and my husband fight in battle, whose side should I be on?" Faced with such a dilemma, even the queen did not know how to answer. So she replied lightly, "It all depends on you."

In Buddhist history, the Buddha also faced a dilemma in his life. He was caught between his mission to benefit and liberate all sentient beings and his right to inherit the throne. He had to choose between duty to his family and renouncing home life to cultivate himself. However, he met with his former wife, Yasodhara, after he attained Buddhahood and told her resolutely, "Though I have let you down, I have not let all sentient beings down."

Among cultivated monks, Venerable Master Kumarajiva was outstanding. He also faced serious dilemmas in his life. He was forced by a warlord to marry a princess in order to save the citizens of his country. In addition, in the course of his cultivation he had to make a choice between Theravada practice and the Mahayana path of bodhisattvas.

In Christianity, there are many examples of saints and martyrs, such as Jesus and Copernicus, who sacrificed their lives for their beliefs. Today some young people want to realize their ideal to affirm their faith, and choose to become monastics. However, they are often caught in the dilemma of parental objection and the need to support their family financially.

There are several hundred thousand Malaysians living in Singapore. The people of Singapore ask them, "If one day Singapore and Malaysia go to war, will you be on the side of Singapore or Malaysia?"

In reality, there are many dilemmas in life. When faced with a dilemma, we need not try to resolve it quickly. We should allow time to ease all situations, transforming crisis into opportunities. It is more ideal to reach a win-win situation. Turning a dilemma into joy for all concerned is the perfect solution.

THE KARMA OF KILLING

The most serious wrongdoing in the world is killing. Since all sentient beings have a life, how can anyone take it away from another? How can we allow others to suffer while we enjoy life?

While the karma from killing is very serious, there are times when it can be forgiven. For instance, unintentional killing is looked upon by a court of law as a much lesser offense. As for those who kill with intention, commit suicide, ask another to kill or kill needlessly, they all carry serious karma. We should not kill animals like pigs, horses, cows, sheep, fish, shrimp or shellfish unjustifiably, because they also have the right to live and thus need to be protected. However, in today's society, people eat live fish, young pigeons, suckling pigs, etc., in the name of gourmet dining. With the persistence of such karma of killing, how can social trends be benevolent and kind? There is a saying, "If you want to know what the battlefield is like, with its guns and swords, just listen to the slaughterhouses at night."

There are other kinds of killing as well. When we discard a usable garment after only wearing it once, or we needlessly throw out chairs and tables that can still be used, we are also killing or wasting natural resources. Parents who do not teach their children to cherish life let them play with bugs such as ants, moths or dragonflies, killing them in the process. If they allow their children to jump up and down on the family sofa, ruining it within a short time, they are also killing life.

It is not always necessary to kill with guns and knives. Some people kill by not treasuring time. They loiter around all day, not doing any work, allowing time to slip by. Since life loses its meaning and value, they are killing their own lives. Thus, killing time is also killing lives.

Others kill through their words. They speak with tongues sharper than a knife, or write to expose other people's secrets and damage their good name. In addition, many people like to gossip, spreading rumors or wrecking families and ruining others' marriages. This not only kills individuals but also destroys families. The latter is far more serious.

The ugliest act of humanity is killing each other. Throughout

history, power-mongers have waged wars and battles to satisfy their ambitions, killing and maiming numerous living beings. So what value is there if war is won but life is lost?

When the Qing Dynasty overturned the Ming Dynasty, there were massacres in several regions for days. So what was there to gain for the descendants of the Manchurians afterwards? Germany killed millions of Jews during World War II, and the Japanese massacred hundreds of thousands of Chinese in Nanjing. These cruel acts only provoked fear in people.

No country should indulge in the serious karma of killing, and no one should engage in killing animals for long. Both governments and average people should stop the bad habit and karma of killing before it is too late. "Bodhisattvas fear causes, and sentient beings fear effects." We should never wait for the rude awakening of karmic retribution before we are enlightened to the harm of the karma of killing.

WHY?

When people talk with one another, the word they use most often is "why." From childhood, we start asking why this and why that. For example, we ask why the wind blows, why fire burns, why water is cold, and why we get hungry. We are curious about everything.

After we are grown, we learn to care for others. We ask, "Why did you come here today? Is there anything I can do for you? Have you eaten yet? Where are you working?" If we start blaming others for things they do, we say, "Why are you so unreasonable? Why are you so selfish? Why are you throwing a tantrum? Why are you late? Why aren't you finished yet? Why aren't you paying back the money you borrowed? Why are you so rude?"

"Why" can also express concern for another. For example: Why did you get sick? Why don't you see a doctor? Why don't you take vitamins to build up your immunity? Why don't you get someone to look after you? "Why" is sometimes used for teaching and inspiring in Chan Buddhism. Questions often asked are: Why are we carrying a corpse everywhere we go? Why can't we see our true face before we were born? Why do we carry such a heavy stone in our hearts? Why should we discuss living and dying? Why did you wait until today to come over?

The many inventions of scientists are the result of asking why and questioning the many phenomena around us. Isaac Newton was curious about why apples fall from trees and discovered gravity. James Watts wondered why steam lifts the lid off a pot when something is cooking and invented the steam engine. Benjamin Franklin saw flashes of thunder and lightning and discovered electricity. The Wright brothers were astonished by the way birds flew and invented airplanes.

When people are confronted with issues they cannot accept, they air their dissatisfaction by yelling, "Why? Why?" Before ruling on a case, the judge first asks many questions. Some people don't know how to ask why, and many others cannot provide an answer. Those who ask why are people who think and have a

point of view and understanding. Therefore, Buddhism teaches, "Small doubts bring small enlightenment, big doubts bring major enlightenment, and no doubt brings no enlightenment."

People should have questions, especially when there are so many whys in the world. They may ask why bamboo and trees can be made into paper, why oil is derived from soybeans and sesame seeds when pressed, why mules are born from a horse and donkey, and why people have different color skin. Those who answer the questions sometimes give the wrong explanations or irrelevant reasons, and the ones who ask may only come to understand the surface of an issue, not the full reality. In the end why is still why, and nothing is solved.

Eastern people learn to accept everything completely. On the other hand, Western people always like to ask why when they are learning. Those who ask why usually do not give up until they find the truth.

When Eastern people talk, they often use why to blame others: Why are you like this? Why are you like that? In dealing with others, Western people do not like too many question marks. They like to use "periods" when they talk: I already ate. I already did it. I already saw it. Everything is completed.

"Why" is something we use broadly in life, but how we use it is a major study in and of itself. Therefore, we should think deeply before using the word why.

MORPHING

Everything in the world is in constant flux. Mountains, rivers, men, and women all morph on a daily basis. In addition, the languages, cultures, traditions, social mores, and habits of every place in the world also morph and improve with time.

There is nothing that does not change. For instance, in physics, when a neutron is emitted from an atom, it transforms into another atom. In nature, worms develop into moths and butterflies, while cicadas and snakes shed their skin as they grow. Every stage in life represents change. A baby girl grows into a young lady, marries and becomes a mother and eventually a senior. So everything in the world is impermanent, as the nature of life is endless changes.

Since everything is in constant change, if a person is too attached to his or her ways, sticking with the old and refusing to improve, no one can help him or her. Therefore, the Buddha said, "I am like a skillful guide showing people the best way. If you do not take the right path, the fault is not with the guide. I am like a proficient doctor prescribing the right medicine for the illness. If you do not take the prescription, the mistake is not with the doctor."

We go to school to be educated in order to change our temperament. We also need to change the surroundings we live and work in, so we change residences and jobs during our lives. With change comes progress. This is illustrated in the educational system a country establishes. Our future success starts with attending kindergarten, moving on to elementary and then high school, and eventually progressing to college and university. In the end, we may become a scholar or professional, such as a teacher, doctor, engineer, or lawyer.

People often comment, "You are a changed person!" When someone changes from being ignorant to being ethical, we praise him or her as having changed from the inside out. In Chan Buddhism, when a practitioner gains enlightenment, he or she has morphed from the inside out.

There are many changes in the world. Some change for the

better, and others for the worse. In politics, there are frequent reforms in policies and strategies. In a ballgame, pitchers are trained to throw curveballs. When propagating the Dharma, changing the wording is a skillful means. In traditional Chinese opera, there is a genre in which the actor changes his or her face on stage. "*Face Off*" is a popular Hollywood movie in which the lead actor changed into a different person. Changes can indeed be astonishing and moving.

Some changes are easy and natural, such as playing a song in one key and modulating to another, or green leaves turning into brilliant oranges and reds. When people change their minds, it may cause much sorrow and pain to others. A good heart changes for the worse, but a wicked mind can also change for the better. Greed, anger and delusion can be changed into the precepts, meditative concentration, and wisdom. However, if one fails to improve on the latter three and does not progress through diligence, when adverse conditions arise, the person can relapse into greed, anger, and delusion.

Therefore, once there is change, what follows will definitely be different. It is best for us to change greed to generosity, anger to compassion, and delusion to wisdom. As long as our minds can morph for the better, then it will not be difficult for us to become a sage or enlightened person!

MAIN AND SUPPORTING ROLES

It is almost time for the Oscars. On a night of red carpet and movie stars, the Academy will announce the year's winners for Best Picture, Best Director, Best Supporting Actor, Best Supporting Actress, Best Actor, Best Actress, Best Screenplay, Best Sound Effects, and so forth. Why does the Academy recognize those who do not have leading roles in a movie? They do it because without their support a picture would never make it to the big screen. In other words, the production of a movie is a collective effort.

To be a major player has nothing to do with our status or position. For example, the three men who became sworn brothers in the Epoch of the Three Kingdoms were not principal figures. It was Zhuge Liang who assumed the principal role, with the masterful scheme to develop a triangular balance of power. In the *Romance of the West Chamber*, one of the most famous Chinese dramas, the hero and heroine would not have been united without the help of the maid, who turned out to be the heart and soul of the story. Although Song Emperor Ren was a virtuous ruler, people today do not know much about his reign, except for the righteous deeds of Bao Zheng, who was an upright official known for his impartial interpretation of the laws and unwillingness to sacrifice their integrity. So, as the saying goes, "Life is like a play, and a play is like life." In real life situations, we do not need to be a big shot in order to be a main player. As long as we adequately fulfill our roles, we can turn the tables and take the lead.

In reality, a supporting role is not necessarily inferior to a leading one. However, in real life it is not easy for people to play second fiddle. Some professional women complain about their supporting roles and being unappreciated in their organizations because they are compared to a vase, beautiful but useless. But a vase, though not a major piece of furniture, has its own value and purpose in adorning a room, making it more pleasing and tasteful. If the vase were to become indispensable, it would succeed in its supporting role.

Some people say that there is always a good and dutiful wife

behind every great man. In this scenario, the husband is the main character and the wife plays a supporting role. However, according to the law of causation, without a good supporting actress, there may not be a good leading role.

Although a lotus flower is beautiful, the green background of its leaves helps to enhance its brilliance even more. In this world, when we consider politicians or popular entertainers, we should not only enjoy their attractive appearance, but also recognize the skills of their support staff. In a big corporation, it is easier to be the president than the general manager, because it is more difficult for someone in a supporting role. The same goes for many civic groups, where it is easier to be on the board of directors than to be the secretary general. This is, indeed, the value of a supporting role.

If a person actually has the ability to be the main character, he or she should also be willing to play a supporting role, and vice versa. If we are to be capable of great achievements, we must be able to wear different hats at different times. A parent is successful if he or she has the skills of a family leader when the children are young, and is willing to give up that role when the children are grown. It is understandable that everyone aspires to be a main player, but when that goal is unattainable, we simply play our own roles the best we can. Being in a supporting role is as valuable as being in a leading role.

THE FOUR VIEWS OF WATER

According to the Buddhist teaching of the Yogacara school, the universe is the manifestation of cognition, and all phenomena change with the mind. The theory of "four views of water" is a testimony to this teaching. Water is something every being can see. Whether it is an ocean, river or brook, humans see it as water. However, heavenly beings see it as crystal. For hungry ghosts, it is seen as pus and blood. For fish and other beings that live in water, it is home and heaven.

Why do humans see water as water, while beings from other realms see it differently? It is because of differences in People's karmic effects. People's tastes vary according to the individual. Some enjoy sour lemons while others cannot stand them. Some love the pungent durian while others cannot take it. Some relish spicy jalapenos while others will not even touch them. Because of people's different karmic effects, what they see and like are also different.

All living beings have different characters, behaviors, forms, preferences, and views. For example, some enjoy literature, some are attracted to philosophy, some love art, and some are fascinated by science. In choosing a place to live, some prefer the mountains, some the waterfront, some the open fields, and some the city. In pursuing a career, some bury themselves in studies, some make as much money as they can, some pursue politics, and some dedicate themselves to religion. However, our many differences are neither good nor bad. If they are accepted as the "four views of water," everyone can coexist peacefully.

Parents today often make demands on their children according to their own views. This is similar to forcing someone who does not like spicy food to have a plate of hot chili or someone who does not have a sweet tooth to eat caramel fudge. It is like trying to convince an urban dweller to live in the countryside, or a nature-lover to move into the heart of town. Such actions are counter to the character of the person and, accordingly, are difficult for him or her to follow. The results are naturally undesirable.

Some people pay a lot of attention to the way they dress but

not to how they eat. Some indulge themselves in gourmet food but do not care about their living environment, whereas others value a comfortable home but not what they wear or eat. Chan Buddhism encourages people to follow their circumstances and expand their own nature. When we all live according to our values and tastes, we can truly live happy and wonderful lives.

RESPECT DISSIDENT

No two people always share the same opinions. As long as there are two or more people involved in any matter, their opinions will differ. Children born from the same mother have different personalities. China has a population of 1.3 billion, and there are certainly as many minds. There is water in brooks, rivers and oceans, but the water quality and movement are not the same. Similarly, none of the hills and mountains in the world is identical. Our thumbs and fingers have different lengths, our two eyes may differ in size, and the teeth in our mouths are all different. People may have the same last name or come from the same school, office or town, but there are many differences within the similarities they share!

There are different branches of the armed forces: the Army, Navy, and Air Force. Among religions, there are Buddhism, Taoism, Christianity, Islam, Judaism, and so forth. There are different types of literature, such as prose, poetry, and the novel. In philosophy, there are Western and Eastern schools, as well as ancient and contemporary thought. There are many things in the world that are more different than similar. The way to approach the world, therefore, is to look for similarities within the differences, and vice versa. How do we live with the many differences in the world? The only way is through respect, tolerance and cooperation, and the sharing of responsibilities. These are not easy to practice. This is the way to conduct oneself in life. It is also the greatest challenge for us in the universe.

Renowned Chinese scholar Liang Qichao once said, "The me of today is declaring war on the me of yesterday." We see here that "the me" of yesterday is different from "the me" of today! Yesterday's lovers may become today's enemies. People do not want to be with people or things that are different from them. As the saying goes, "Those who go my way may live, and those who oppose me should be banished." We want to get rid of all that we find disagreeable. However, there are more than tens of thousands of people and things in this world that are different from us, so how can we possibly do away with all of them? Since we cannot

get rid of them all, the best way to cope with reality is to have mutual respect and tolerance. In respecting dissidents, we act in accord with the law of the universe.

We all know that fire and water do not mix, but in southern Taiwan there is a ridge where water and fire share the same source. Peaches and plums are different fruits, but they can be crossed to produce nectarines. Men and women are clearly different, but they often say they have each other inside themselves. The colors of the rainbow are varied, but because they do not reject each other their beauty is especially distinctive.

When our eyes cannot see what is happening on the other side of the wall, our ears may help us hear the sounds. What we cannot move with our feet, we may push with our hands. When there is a drought, we hope for rain, and when it rains too much, we long for sunshine. Water can support a ship and also overturn it. Fire can evaporate water, but water can put out fire. All things in the world coexist by mutual benefit and restraint.

As long as there are two people, there will always be arguments. It is impossible to have perfect unity. Therefore, though we are different, we should respect each other. By having mutual respect, we can all coexist in peace!

THE CRISIS OF NOT UNDERSTANDING SUFFERING

In modern society, great progress has been made toward being alert for crises. Those who do not have a sense of danger live their lives in delusion and are completely unprepared for any calamity or suffering. For example, in the old days, Chinese guarded their homes with heavy doors and shutters to prevent invasion.

Suffering is a reality of life. As long as we live in this world, none of us can escape the test of suffering. We suffer the cold and heat of weather changes, hunger or bloating from eating, warmth and indifference in relationships, or aging and death. If we do not understand suffering, we remain ignorant of the world in which we live and the art of building relationships.

If we understand suffering, we can be better prepared. When we are healthy, we should know the suffering of sickness, and when we are still young, we should understand the pains of old age. Through our understanding of suffering, we will know how to deal with its problems when we do suffer. By living through the changing seasons, we feel impermanence. Therefore, we should cherish life and make the best use of time. We should finish what we need to do on time, because when impermanence rears its head, our lives may end in regret. By understanding the suffering of birth, sickness, aging, death and impermanence, we can prepare in advance. By knowing aging, we cherish youthfulness, and by understanding sickness and death, we learn to befriend our illnesses and even look upon death as returning home. We will no longer fear it.

As humans, we should understand how difficult it is for us to take care of every aspect of our lives and work. If we realize our limitations, then we can appreciate the emptiness of all phenomena, as they only arise and cease due to conditions.

While there are matters that we need not know about, there are things that we should know. For instance, we should not forget when others help us, and we should know the reason why others become angry with us. If we do not handle our relationships and situations skillfully, we fail to appreciate the danger and suf-

fering around us. Then, we would live a dangerous life indeed.

When it is going to rain, we should get our umbrellas handy, and when a snowstorm is imminent, we should stock up on food and fuel. The world's economy is unstable, so we should save up for a rainy day. Human hearts can be vicious and devious; however, we still need to respect one another. If we are ignorant, we will be devastated when faced with the bitter fruit of suffering.

There is a saying, "We can know people's faces but not their hearts." In reality, people in this world "Know the world and its joys but not the suffering." Understanding suffering is the condition we must meet for us to progress on the Way. The glory of success in this world is the result of a lot of hard work and perseverance. If we do not know suffering, we do not know the importance of diligence. Therefore, it is often difficult for those with fame and fortune to learn the Way. It is so important for us to understand suffering, because in doing so we will not be swept away by the currents of life.

QUESTION MARKS

Some people like to use periods when they speak; others prefer exclamation marks and ellipses, while some like question marks. Those who like periods will give an answer or explanation about anything. People who like ellipses will let you know what they are talking about, as long as you ask them. Those who like to use exclamation marks like to make a fuss over little or nothing. Those who like to speak with question marks find what they try to say to be complicated.

Question marks sometimes connote care and concern and eventually lead to good answers, but at other times they bring about poor results. For instance, when asking about others, we might say: How have you been? Have you eaten? How are your folks doing? These are benevolent questions. Sometimes, others may ask for opinions: What do you think of the world situation right now? What is your opinion of the economy? Do you agree with what the president is doing? These are neutral questions without implication. The worst questions imply blame such as: What are you doing here? Why haven't you finished your work yet? Why did you spend so much money? Why are you eating so much? Why are you late today? When we talk to others in such a tone, the reply we get is unpredictable.

We know we are in trouble if we are asked questions like: Are you reliable? Can you be trusted? Are you qualified? Can you carry this responsibility? If we have a poor track record, people may ask: Didn't you oppose this project initially? Didn't you fight with your coworkers before? You left your post without notice, didn't you? Do you remember that you did not complete your work? Therefore, once we become a person under interrogation, others find it difficult to trust us.

However, we should be able to stand up to different types of questions and give positive, satisfactory answers to anyone who asks them. If we can do this, we will be able to gain a firm position in any organization or society.

We need not ask questions all the time, because being positive about things is often much better. When someone wants our

help, we should not say, "Why don't you do it yourself?" When someone wants to borrow a book from us, we can either refuse or tell the person we do not have it, but we often ask, "Why don't you go buy one yourself?" When people want to borrow money, we can simply refuse, but we should not ask, "Why do you always borrow money?" If we carry on conversations with others in this manner, it only serves to damage our relationships with them.

There is an art to asking questions. The art of questioning should be done with respect and humility, especially when asking for help. There should not be any implication of finding fault or answering a question with another question, because no matter how good our intentions may be, we will not be artful in the way we speak.

In the *Record of the Warring States*, there were many dialogues between emperors and other emperors; ministers and other ministers; emperors and their own ministers; and even debates between lobbyists of the time. The ethics and wisdom contained within their questions and answers are limitless. They provide the best examples for us to learn from. We should accept others as teachers, scholars and experts, and in doing so we will be able to gain wisdom from our conversations.

LAWS AND PRINCIPLES

A law is formulated when a phenomenon is universal and inevitable. Birth, sickness, old age, and death are the laws of life. Existence, decay, and emptiness are the laws of the world. Impermanence and change are the laws of natural phenomena. Laws are formulations based on certainty and universality and cannot be changed without justification.

Throughout the ages, philosophers from both the East and West have formulated many theories concerning the meaning of life and the existential nature of the universe. Scientists past and present have tried to derive a pattern of certainty and universality from their discoveries and observations. Einstein's Theory of Relativity, Newton's Law of Gravity, and Darwin's Theory of Evolution, that explains survival of the fittest through the Law of Natural Selection, are examples of how scientists have tried to explain nature and the workings of the universe.

However, not every theory or hypothesis can withstand the test of time and thus be classified as truth. As science has become more advanced, many early scientific theories and principles have lost their validity. They have become footnotes to a better and more advanced theory of science, subject to change and impermanence, and limited by the conditions of time and space.

According to the Buddha's teachings, nothing in life or the universe can exist without the requisite conditions, as each cause produces an inevitable effect. This is the law of cause and effect. Every phenomenon is subject to causality, and this is the law of nature. Since all phenomena occur through conditions and all that come into being are dependent on something else, the doctrine of dependent origination is the law of interdependent relationships. It is upon realization of the laws concerning life and the universe that the Buddha attained perfect enlightenment. He discovered that "every effect comes from a cause or a set of causes," "every phenomenon occurs by means of conditions," "all matters depend on logic," "multiplicity is born of singularity," "existence is dependent on emptiness," and "Buddhahood is attained by beings of the human realm."

If we put aside the ultimate truth of Buddhism and instead focus attention on laws related to human existence, it will be difficult to find a person who is well known by oneself. When respect and compliments are demanded, the laws of human sentiment are at work. When an abundance of daily provisions is pursued, the laws of livelihood prevail. When fame, fortune and power are desired, the laws of wealth are operating. When health and longevity are emphasized, the law of self-centeredness dominates.

There are also laws concerning the intricacies of human relationships, such as love, hate, intimacy, and alienation. If we understand most of them, we will be able to minimize conflicts and avoid misunderstandings. However, some people have yet to grasp the laws of relationships, causing them to confuse the good with the bad and the significant with the insignificant. This failure to understand the principles behind the laws of human interaction can lead to chaos or disorder.

Time can be divided into the three periods of past, present, and future in accordance with the law of circularity. The spatial directions of east, south, west, and north have the laws of orientation as their compass. Even the sun and moon have their own laws of motion, where the Earth revolves around the sun and the moon is a satellite of the Earth.

We must have a firm grasp of the laws of life and death, happiness and suffering, and human relationships in our lives. If we can understand the laws of interdependency, that which is harmful and trivial will not deceive us. When will the wind blow and the rain pour down? Why is spring gentle and winter harsh? In what ways are our loved ones happy and our friends dissatisfied? If we know the answers to these questions, we will have little trouble understanding the laws of life and the universe, and conduct ourselves successfully in this world.

IMMUNITY

Today, there are security guards on duty around the clock in some communities or apartment buildings to keep thieves, vagrants, and other undesirables from entering the premises without permission and threatening the safety of the residents. Our physical bodies also have an immune system that prevents the invasion of viruses and germs that may harm our health.

In its simplest form, immunity is an antibody that can fight invasion from the outside. Within a healthy body, there are many good viruses that can fight and kill the bad ones. For instance, when we are stressed and tired, it is easy to catch the flu. For those who have sufficient antibodies, a little stress or cold will not affect them in a major way. However, without the proper antibodies, we easily contract diseases such as pneumonia, hepatitis or malaria; but if we produce the antibodies to fight these ailments, we will have immunity from them.

According to research, about ninety percent of the sicknesses that we are infected with result from a weakened immune system. The immune system is like a well-trained army, safeguarding the health of the human body. Besides protecting it from disease, a strong immune system supports the functioning of the body as it cleans out metabolic wastes and repairs damaged organs and tissues.

Doctors usually make use of various drugs to enhance the immune systems of their patients. They also instruct their patients in ways to achieve better health, such as getting sufficient sleep, at least thirty minutes of exercise a day, body massages, laughing heartily, relaxing the body and mind, and taking vitamins. These all help improve immunity. Dr. Herbert Benson of Harvard University Medical School indicated that people with religious faith are generally healthier than those without it.

Our bodies need the help of a healthy immune system to fight disease, and our minds require antibodies to prevent the invasion of different viruses such as gossip, pornography, gains, losses, and right and wrong. If our immunity is not strong enough, we will be seriously harmed. So we need to fortify our immune system.

Practitioners need prajna-wisdom to overcome ignorance and delusion, the antibody of Chan mindfulness to counter distractions, and the antidote of the precepts to rid themselves of faults they should not commit. Precepts, concentration, and wisdom are every practitioner's antibodies.

In Buddhism, bodhisattvas and cultivated practitioners have a strong immune system from their practice. Ksitigarbha Bodhisattva went into the hell realm to liberate the beings there and emerged untainted. Avalokitesvara Bodhisattva traveled freely throughout the world without fear of attacks from evil and relieved sentient beings of their suffering; Vimalakirti went to saloons and brothels to teach people the Dharma. If a Chan practitioner cannot teach and help people on busy streets and be equipped with immunity against distractions, how can he or she be a Chan practitioner?

In the first World Cup Soccer Game in Asia, the of us of each team alertly guarded every corner of their goal posts so that their opponents could not kick the ball in. All goalkeepers should have this level of skillfulness and immunity to safeguard against invasion.

Society is filled with so many diseases and distractions. Without strong immunity, we will be in harm's way. Therefore, we need to be wary and fortify our physical and spiritual immune systems.

LEARN A LESSON

We may have learned numerous lessons throughout our lives but still failed to make progress. However, if we are enlightened by another's words or actions, the lesson we learn will influence our entire life.

Some people explore the deep ocean, going through different kinds of dangers and learning lessons. Mountain climbers use their wisdom to conquer high peaks and learn a lesson in life. Many people travel to various places in the world, gain much knowledge about different regions, cultures, and customs and learn a precious lesson.

Confucius said, "I am not as good as an old farmer" because he learned a lesson from one. In Buddhism, Chan masters were often able to enlighten seekers of the Way with a few words, in order for the students to learn an important lesson in life.

Once a student went to a temple to learn Chan but later decided to leave. The Chan master asked, "Where do you want to go?"

The student replied, "I want to learn."

The Chan master asked, "What are you learning?"

"I am learning 'Mind Only.'"

The Chan master said, "The Three Realms are within our mind, and all dharmas are from consciousness. Is this rock by the road in the mind or outside?"

The student explained, "In the mind."

The Chan master said, "Why do you have to be so hard on yourself? Why place a big rock in your mind?"

On hearing that, the student became enlightened.

Chan Master Desan studied the *Diamond Sutra* deeply and wrote a commentary on it. He heard about the practice of "instant enlightenment" advocated in the South but thought little of it. Traveling south, he brought his writings, with the goal of criticizing the deviant teaching. When he reached the south, he passed a small shop selling dim sum. Since he was hungry, he decided to stop for a snack. The old woman in the store learned that the Chan Master considered himself an expert on the *Diamond Sutra* and asked, "It is said in the *Diamond Sutra*: 'The past mind cannot be found, the present mind cannot be grasped, and the future mind cannot be detected.' So, Chan Master, you want to eat dim sum;

what kind of mind is that?" The Chan Master was at a loss for an answer. (In Chinese, "dim" means pointing at, and "sum" means heart and also mind.)

A scholar once saw a couplet on the wall of a temple: "Mt. Sumero embraces a mustard seed; a mustard seed contains Mt. Sumero." He was skeptical and commented, "It is understandable to say Mt. Sumero embraces a mustard seed. But how can a tiny mustard seed contain Mt. Sumero? This couplet does not make sense." The Chan master there replied, "There is a saying 'After going through ten thousand volumes of books, one can write like a god.' So how do you store ten thousand volumes of books inside a small belly?" The scholar became enlightened on hearing this.

In the Buddha's time, the kingdom of Magadha wanted to invade Vrji, so its king sent his minister Varsakara to consult the Buddha to find out if they should forge ahead with the battle. The Buddha did not reply directly but asked his attendant Ananda, "Ananda! Have you heard that the citizens of Vrji live orderly lives honoring their parents and teachers?"
Ananda replied, "Yes."

The Buddha explained, "Exactly! This kingdom is solid as rock and not easy to overcome."

He asked again, "Ananda! Have you heard that their citizens uphold the law and strictly observe the precepts?"

Ananda replied, "Yes."

The Buddha further explained, "Exactly! This kingdom is solid as rock and not easy to overcome."

The Buddha asked seven similar questions and received seven answers. Varsakara then knew the answer. This lesson preserved the security of a country.

Tang scholar Han Yu once paid Chan Master Dadian a visit. The Chan Master was in deep meditative concentration and remained immobile. His attendant commented, "First move with concentration; then teach with wisdom." On hearing that, Han couldn't help but exclaim, "I already got the message from the attendant!" Mr. Han Yu learned his lesson from the attendant's words.

There is a saying, "Speaking with the wise is worth more than studying for ten years." As long as we pay attention, there are similar lessons in life everywhere we go.

IMAGINATION

People are born with imagination. It is the driving force behind progress. If people did not have imagination, the world would be blank and life very boring. Therefore, we must teach young students to imagine in order for them to create as they grow up. Even if they fail, it is still all right because it is only with imagination that they can possibly succeed in turning their dreams and goals into reality.

Imagination is often inspired by reality. For instance, the Wright brothers invented airplanes after they saw birds fly. Chan masters watched flowers bloom and wither and realized the truths of impermanence, suffering, and emptiness. They all had imagination. If Newton had lacked imagination when he saw all the apples fall from a tree, he would not have felt anything or discovered gravity. Therefore, creativity depends on imagination.

Landing people on the moon also took imagination. Because of imagination, Neil Armstrong's one small step meant a giant leap for humanity and allowed people to see the true face of the moon. Impressionist painters completed many art pieces with their imagination. However, most people fail to appreciate the art within. It also takes imagination to truly understand our inner messages. While many people made pen pals in the old days, now people often meet friends on the Internet instead. Either way, we rely on imagination to keep the friendships going because if people were to meet their pen pals or Internet friends in person, they would often be hugely disappointed.

Children and poets probably have the most imagination. Writers, especially those who write science fiction and detective stories, need a very good imagination. There are classic stories filled with imaginary wonder, such as *Alice in Wonderland*, *Snow White*, and *Harry Potter*, and Chinese tales such as "*Journey to the West*," "*Chang Er Flew to the Moon,*" and Tao Yuan Ming's "*Peach Flower Spring*." The ancients even "drew a piece of cake to fill their hunger" and "looked at plums to quench their thirst." The virtual reality of the Internet is also the result of imagination.

Scientists invent many things based on imagination.

However, in their courage to imagine and hypothesize, they still need to prove their ideas with great caution. Many people nowadays are full of imagination. Novelists and playwrights often leave much room for audiences to draw their own conclusions and visualize. In this way, audiences can use their own imagination and realize their dreams through the stories.

People are great because they dare to dream. Dreaming is based on imagination, and it is through imagination that life can be colorful and exciting.

LOST

After we come to understand the ways of the world and set goals in life, there are many different ways to reach them. When we travel, for example, we can take a plane, train or car, or even walk to our destination. It is similar for our goals in life because we can reach them regardless of the means of transportation. The difference only lies in the amount of time used. However, if we become lost, then we will not be able to reach our goals.

There are a number of reasons for us to get lost in the course of life. For example, bad weather conditions, difficult terrain, darkness, delusion, temptation, fear, injuries, lack of courage, and obstacles in the form of high mountains or large rivers. It is easier for us to handle external problems, for as long as we have the right company, questions and instruments, a compass and map, we can find our way. However, it is very difficult to move forward when we are lost in thinking, such as confused, have attachments, delusion, fantasy, ignorance, indecisiveness, and misjudgment. These are the reasons we become lost on the path of life.

Mountain climbers do not fear heights or hot and cold climates. They fear being lost. Seafarers have no fear of giant oceans, waves and wind. Losing direction is what they are afraid of. Likewise, the pilot of a plane can easily manage darkness and long distances, but his worry is going off the flight course. Young people today often become attached to the beautiful vistas on the path of life and become lazy, refusing to work hard. They easily lose their temper, get moody and indulge in romance, losing sight of their goals and future. Middle-aged people may be sidelined by poor choice of friends, and cheated of their savings and even their careers. Older people sometimes are unclear about where they should reside in their later years and are uncertain of their livelihood. They lose direction in the final stage of life, not knowing where to turn.

Venerable Master Xuanzhuang of the Tang Dynasty relied on concentration in order to stay on course through the long miles of quicksand in the desert. Christopher Columbus depended on courage and faith to seek out a new continent. Renowned Han

ambassador Zhang Qian relied on perseverance to establish the historic Silk Road. The Dutch employed their wisdom of the ocean in the fight for land.

Are we fearful of getting lost? We need a map to help us. It comes in the form of teachers, benevolent and knowledgeable friends, and our seniors. They are familiar with the way, they can guide us onto the right path. In addition, a compass can show us the direction, and history and the truth can help us tell the difference between right and wrong. If we ignite the light in our hearts, we can shine it on the path of life. Religion, right views, courage, preparation, good health, physical strength, and integrity can all lead us in the right direction. When we have sound knowledge of the physical terrain in front of us, we can avoid obstacles. If we make broad connections with people, then even when we get lost, there will be people to show us the way back to where we started.

The Buddha said, "I am like the knowledgeable guide directing people onto the right path. Whether they take it or not is not the fault of the guide." Therefore, those of us who are lost should realize that our parents, teachers, and prominent figures in society have already opened the road of life to us, and we should not become lost on it!

ORGAN TRANSPLANTS

There is an interesting old Buddhist story relevant to today's practice of transplanting organ. Once a traveler missed the opportunity to check into an inn and stayed at a deserted temple for the night. In the middle of the night, a little ghost came into the temple carrying a body. The traveler was terrified and thought, "There's a ghost in here!" Just then a big ghost entered, pointed at the little one and asked, "Why are you carrying the body that I found?" The little ghost replied, "It's mine. Why do you say it's yours?" As the two ghosts fought and haggled over the body, the traveler shook uncontrollably in horror, and the noise he made caught the attention of the little ghost. "Ha!" said the little ghost, "Someone is hiding under the shrine. Come out! Don't be afraid! Judge for us whose body this is!"

The traveler thought there was no way he could escape, and if he was going to die anyway, he should tell the truth. Bravely he said, "The body belongs to the little ghost!" Upon hearing this, the big ghost was so angry that he dashed up and ripped the left arm off the man and ate it in three bites. The little ghost thought, "This man is on my side. I must help him." So immediately he pulled the left arm off the body and replaced the traveler's arm. The big ghost was still upset, so he ripped off the man's right arm and ate it in three more bites. The little ghost again replaced it with the right arm from the body. This went on for a while. After the big ghost ate the man's right leg, the little ghost replaced it with the right leg from the body and so on. After both ghosts finished fighting, they left without a trace. The poor man was left alone and puzzled, "Who am I now?"

This is one of the fables in Buddhism that defines the meaning of "The four basic elements are empty and the five components of existence have no self." However, the story also illustrates the benefits of organ transplants.

Organ transplants are a major achievement in modern medical science. They offer many dying people a new opportunity for life. At the same time, the compassion of the organ donor lives on in the world. This represents the giving of one's internal wealth.

In his previous lives, the Buddha cut off his flesh to feed a hawk and offered himself to a hungry tigress. Through diligent practice and bearing the near impossible, the Buddha set an example for us to live by over two thousand years ago.

Today, by donating our body parts, we can recycle the organs we no longer have use for and give our love to others still living in the world. When we give a cornea, we bring brightness. When we give a heart, we offer the drive for life. When we give bone marrow, we pour the stream of our life into another. Organ transplants give others the opportunity for life and also extend our lifeline. They break the border between self and others and the Chinese superstition of maintaining a complete body at death.

Organ transplants embody true compassion and the sharing of life with our kind. As long as there is the will, we are all capable of donating our organs. Through organ transplants, we can extend and broaden our compassion and love endlessly.

WHAT IS LEFT BEHIND?

When parents leave for work in the morning, what food do they leave for their children? When doctors get off work, what kind of care do they leave behind for their patients? When people immigrate to another place, what do they leave behind for their friends and relatives? When family elders pass away, what is left for the younger generations? Some people live off an inheritance from their parents or grandparents to keep up a good life. Others rely on themselves.

Our Chinese ancestors left us a wealth of culture in the form of numerous literary collections, chronologies of the dynasties, the twelve divisions of the Tripitaka, Chan Koans, and teachings of the saints and sages. These are immortal gifts. In addition, they planted fields, hillside forests, canals, tunnels, roads and trails, which all have provided immeasurable convenience for generations to follow. The carvings in caves and mountains, magnificent architecture, and an ancient culture enrich our lives, wisdom, and capabilities.

Our predecessors left us such rich resources. What should we leave for the generations to come? Confucianism indicates that we should leave the three immortals to the world: merit, morals, and writings. Christianity says we should leave love behind. Buddhism teaches that we should share compassion and liberation with everyone!

"Giving" contributes immensely to the present world, and "leaving" lends deep meaning to future generations. Not only do we have to give now, but we also must plan for what we will leave behind in the future. We should leave history, faith, compassion, our contributions, and wisdom to the world. We are not here only to consume and enjoy the world's resources. We need to add to its color, motivation, joy, and culture.

Men and women pass down inheritances to their children, and teachers leave wisdom and skills to their students. Many other people leave something behind for society: scientists leave inventions, philosophers their thinking, farmers leave agricultural experiences, gardeners the fragrance of flowers and plants, politicians

the benefits of their policies, and philanthropists leave their generosity as a role model.

Confucius left behind the four ethics and eight virtues, Zhuangzi the philosophy of no desires and no worries, Zhougung decorum and rituals, da Vinci the smile of Mona Lisa, Beethoven many musical masterpieces, and the Buddha left Buddha Nature and Chan mind. What will you leave behind for the future?

PROBLEM PEOPLE

Who are problem people? They are the uncooperative ones who cause trouble in an organization, object to everything, are unwelcome, create problems, and lack positive human relations. In the past, people who betrayed their country, such as spies and secret agents, and those who were disloyal to their group, were all considered problem people.

It is not easy to assess whether problem people are good or bad. Those who are considered a problem by the benevolent are naturally negative, but those considered a problem by people with unpopular views and questionable intentions may not necessarily be so.

In general, if someone is labeled "a problem," he or she is disliked and usually becomes an extremist. Most people do not want to become problem people, but in reality it is difficult to define anyone as a problem. Many of the Founding Fathers of the United States were considered problem people by the British, but after the nation gained independence, they were honored with great respect.

There are almost always problem people in an organization, family, or school. There are problem workers in factories, problem students in classes, and problem children in families. In fact, anyone can be labeled a problem including: parents, soldiers, politicians, women, and business people. Once identified as a problem, most of them change for the worse and few for the better. Therefore, most people do not want to be viewed as a problem.

In reality, we should become "problem people." Because we all have different thinking, attitudes, actions and views, it is only natural that we have our own problems. If we ask everyone to be problem-free and to say yes to everything, expressing no independent opinions, does it mean everything is fine?

When children are too active, noisy and full of trouble, they may be called problem children. However, when they grow up and work hard, behave properly and become community leaders, will they still be considered problem people? When a young

woman is socially active and good at public relations, she may be criticized as a problem, too. If she is also an advocate for women's rights, who tries to change outdated views of women, promotes gender equality and eventually gains the admiration of women, then she will no longer be considered a problem.

A problem is equal to a question mark with an unknown situation and result. If we are considered a problem, we need not be too concerned. Like a piece of art being sculpted, artistic value cannot be determined until completion. The Chinese often judge a person after he or she passes away, because even problem people can demonstrate a positive example and project a good image. So "problem people" should not be too concerned about how others view them.

WONDER DRUGS

Life is painfully short, so it has driven some people to think of ways to quickly accomplish their goals. While practitioners hope for a shortcut to enlightenment, architects and writers rack their brains for ways to complete projects in the shortest time possible. Similarly, entrepreneurs look for overnight success in their ambitions to become instant millionaires. Even parents anxiously wish for their children to grow up quickly. Because of people's aversion to the idea of gradual progress and the desire for quick results, society has acquired a "fast food" culture, in which instant noodles, ready-to-eat meals, and appliances that guarantee fast cooking time have become increasingly popular. Everywhere we go, we see the promise of instant results, including all kinds of wonder drugs and miracle cures for our ailments.

There is actually no such thing as an instant result or a fast outcome, because everything in the world has come to be in an orderly fashion, one step at a time. If we use chemicals to stimulate the growth of flowers, they will lose their natural fragrance, as they became products of artificiality. If we inject our livestock with growth enhancement hormones, they lose their natural flavors, falling victim to our selfish desire to skirt the natural process. High-speed cars often cause accidents, and fast planes emit too much noise. This emphasis on speed has actually defeated many of our efforts and purposes. The need for immediate efficacy has caused many remedies to lose their effectiveness.

To ask for a quick result or quick relief is to test our luck. When the ancient sages told us that "great talents mature slowly because greatness does not happen overnight," they wanted us to be patient in realizing our full potential so that we could withstand the test of time. For example, an intensive course will not provide a firm foundation in our lessons, because it bypasses the normal process of learning, which requires us to learn step-by-step. When we talk about the Buddhist concept of "sudden enlightenment," what we have in mind is not instant success without effort. It is like eating five bowls of rice, the last of which satisfies our hunger. It is like walking ten miles to reach our destination, the

last step bringing us to our goal.

Everything in this world needs time to grow and mature, and time itself is no exception, because the seconds make up minutes, the minutes make up hours, the hours days, and the slow changes of the four seasons the years. Without proper order and gradual progress, nothing will ever come to be. Without the harshness of winter, a plum blossom will not bloom with its sweet aroma. A child will not grow up to be a normal person if he or she is fed a wonder drug that instantly transforms it into a fifty-something adult. Just imagine a thirty-something parent with a fifty-year-old child! How could they possibly get along when family ethics are ruined?

A farmer will not be able to harvest his rice paddy if the seedlings have not grown and ripened under the summer sun. Nothing on earth will ever come to be without the nourishment of the evening dew. If we are to improve our skills, we must put in the time and effort that are required of us, because there is no perfection without practice. Even in learning a new language, we must let nature take its course, like a newborn baby who naturally learns to talk by the time he or she is two years old. Therefore, "being natural" is still something we should cherish.

The life of our society has been dramatically reduced and the content of our lives distorted because of the need for fast and immediate results. Instant noodles will never satisfy hunger, because they get cold easily. Wonder drugs will not provide long-term relief, because they are full of side effects. Therefore, the best way to succeed in life is to never skip a step, and to follow the proper procedure of cultivation and accumulation.

PUPPET

A former newscaster with CTS (Chinese Television Service) won the Golden Bell Award one year, and after accepting it, raised the trophy and made fun of herself saying, "This is a puppet award!" The term puppet became popular overnight.

A puppet is someone who has no personal views and cannot make decisions because he or she is controlled by another person. Puppets have little spirit or will of their own, and no creative thoughts or self-determination since they are completely controlled by another. By pulling a string, the puppet will dance and prance, and a piece of cloth can make the puppet roll up and down. Someone becomes a puppet when he or she takes bribes, or if another person has a hold on him or her. Someone behind the scene controls all the actions and changes of puppets.

There have been many puppets in the world. The last emperors of every Chinese dynasty were mostly puppets. Today puppets appear in both politics and journalism, fields that do not have their own policies or views about benefiting society but are controlled or used by a minority. In politics, there are ambitious people who purportedly support one politician up front, but who are actually the ones controlling matters from behind. Worse still, there are people willing to be such puppets.

Puppets can even be found in families. Some parents want to control their children's future, making plans for them in the hope that they will follow accordingly. Their children become puppets.

There are many kinds of puppets. Some people sell their self-respect and character for money, fame or power, thus becoming puppets despised by those around them. Others are puppets of words, due to attachment to their ideals and writings, and the refusal to make changes. Some people are attached to tradition and customs, with no intention of changing, improving, or learning anything new. They are puppets of history and tradition.

If we want to live our own lives with dignity and self-respect, we need to cultivate community character, respect for society, and global perspectives from a young age. When we live a life full of passion and justice, we live a life of flesh and blood. Then we will

not be anyone's puppet!

It is loyalty when a subordinate follows direction and guidance from above. However, he or she is a puppet if someone in a high position who has no ideals, abilities or achievements, is using him or her to serve as a front to meet the demands and desires of a minority.

We can only hope that those who are puppets can stand up and live their own lives. They need to be their own masters and not be controlled by others. They should contribute themselves to the community and be used by it in order to transcend the role of a puppet.

KNOWING BOTH GOOD AND BAD

There are both good and bad people in the world. Naturally, we tend to prefer good to bad. However, we should realize that although it is all right to respect good people, we should not turn our backs on the bad ones, because good and bad actually support one another.

The Buddha said, "Lotus flowers do not grow on high plains. They only thrive in low, soggy and muddy swamps." Venerable Master Daoxuan of the Tang Dynasty said, "Benevolence is the teacher of all bad; bad is the source for all benevolence." Laozi taught, "Calamity is what good fortune depends on, and good fortune is where calamity lies in wait. Who can really see through them clearly?" Devadatta was extremely bad and harmed the Buddha on many occasions. However, the Buddha said that he was grateful to Devadatta because he provided the Buddha with the adverse conditions for progress.

Without darkness, we cannot see how important brightness is. When there is no ugliness, beauty will not look so precious. Without bad, how can we appreciate the value of benevolence? When we meet bad people, we naturally distance ourselves from them. However, if we take the initiative to befriend unwholesome elements and transform their malevolence, we will be like sunshine and warm breezes, ripening sour and bitter pineapples and persimmons, and turning them into sweet fruits. Why can't we be sunshine and warm breezes?

Buddhism teaches, "Affliction is bodhi; bodhi is Affliction." We may think that they are not mutually tolerant. In reality, our bodhi mind comes from afflictions and troubles. If we have not seen people suffering in pain, how will compassion arise in us? If we have not witnessed antelope and deer being eaten alive by lions and tigers, how will sympathy grow in our hearts? The bad of the world serves to warn us of the need to be compassionate, just as our worries, indeed, turn into bodhi.

We often hear the saying, "While medicine may be bitter, it cures our sickness; while sound advice may be grating to the ear, it is helpful in our endeavors." How can we get well or improve without taking medicine or without the counsel of others?

Therefore, we should have no fear of defilements and evil, because we learn from them. They provide us examples to reflect on. No matter how unclean the mud is, as long as we can become pure lotus flowers, there is nothing unwholesome about it.

Poisons like arsenic trioxide are harmful to people, but if used appropriately they can also save lives. Morphine and opium are listed as illegal drugs. However, they help kill the pain of cancer and other illnesses. Dynamite kills and maims, but also opens up mountains and rocks. While lies can hurt, they can also save people. These all illustrate the logic and truth behind the relationship between good and bad.

There is no absolute good or bad in the world. While plants and flowers help purify the air and cultivate our body and mind, some plants emit toxic substances that give people allergies. Sunrays provide us with essential vitamins but can also cause skin cancer. Antibiotics kill germs as well as the beneficial bacteria in our system. Appropriate amounts of coffee are beneficial, while excessive amounts cause loss of bone mass. Water relieves thirst, but too much of it may harm the body.

When there is tolerance and loving-kindness, even bad people can attain the Way! This saying illustrates it best: "Put down the butcher knife, and become a Buddha here and now."

BENEVOLENT FRIENDS

Good friends are people who tell us to distance ourselves from all bad deeds and to practice benevolence. They are the guides and teachers we all need to be close to in life.

In a group of people, there are inevitably some benevolent and some unwholesome friends. Benevolent people display and teach ethics, knowledge and skills, while unwholesome ones only lead us into bad deeds, because they have nothing positive about them. With our eye of wisdom, we need to distinguish who is benevolent and who is not.

Examples of benevolent people are our parents who nurture us, teachers who educate us, friends and family members who counsel us, and neighbors who watch out for our safety. In addition, our benevolent "friends" include histories that provide us with lessons that are relevant in today's life, and technology that has helped humanity progress over time. When we read a good book, hear sound advice or come across something positive that brings joy to others and purifies human hearts, we benefit from their benevolence as well. There is a Chan saying, "Clear brooks are broad long tongues; mountains are nothing but pure bodies." Therefore, a flower, a blade of grass, the morning sun, gentle breezes, rain, dew, and the air are all our benevolent friends. The truths taught by Buddhism, such as "suffering," "emptiness," and "impermanence," are all inanimate benevolent friends.

In the *Samyutagama Sutra*, it is written, "Who are the benevolent friends for traveling afar? Who are the benevolent friends at home? Who are the benevolent friends proficient in finance? Who are the benevolent friends for future generations?" The Buddha said, "Merchants are our benevolent friends for traveling afar because in the course of conducting business in many different places, they know where there are resources and scenic views. A chaste and virtuous wife is the benevolent friend at home. Entrepreneurs in the same field working with us to establish our careers are the benevolent friends in finance. When we have right views and understanding, these will be the lasting benevolent friends for future generations."

"In a group of three people, there is always a teacher for me." Since this person is our teacher, he or she is a benevolent friend. Even a foolish person has one capability, and he is our benevolent friend. Confucius once said, "I am not as good as a farmer." Because Confucius did not know how to farm, a farmer was his benevolent friend. By the same token, if we do not how to weave, weavers are our benevolent friends; or if we do not know how to drive, those who do are our benevolent friends. We should understand that all people, matters, and objects that can help improve our character and teach us knowledge and truth are our benevolent friends.

What can we offer these benevolent friends that have provided many causes and conditions to help and support us? Are we willing to respect them with humility, praise them with positive speech, and offer them our service?

If we want to be a benevolent friend, we need to guide others along the right path, be knowledgeable, have right views, be good at teaching, and provide encouragement. When we are able to do so, then we truly understand the path of a benevolent friend.

ALL IS POSSIBLE

When we have a goal to achieve, there are two ways of viewing it. One way is that the goal is "possible;" the other is that it is "impossible." Without resolve and strength, anything that is possible will become impossible. However, for someone with courage, wisdom and a vision, all that seems impossible can become possible. There are many things in the world that will fail if they are handled by people with the "impossible" view. On the other hand, if these matters are dealt with by those who persevere in their pursuits, the goals can surely be reached.

People dreamed of flying like birds in the sky, and now that airplanes have been invented, they can actually be airborne now. People wished to swim in the deep oceans like fish, so they invented the submarine to explore the deep sea. People are willing to mine coal and other minerals buried thousands of feet in the earth. They are capable of climbing to mountain summits over ten thousand feet high. Astronauts have landed on the moon. What other mysteries are there in outer space waiting to be deciphered in the future?

Many patients who have been diagnosed with terminal cancer battle their disease with an uplifting spirit and the determination to live. As a result of their "possible" view, they can regain good health. Nobel Prize laureate Gao Xingjian was a cancer patient. He decided to travel the world after learning of his illness and wrote a book that won him lifelong acclaim. In the final days of the Qin Dynasty, Liu Bang served as a minor local officer. He would never have dreamed of being emperor. However, in the end he founded the Han Dynasty. Likewise, the founding emperor of the Ming Dynasty, Zhu Yuanzhang, was previously a novice monk at a Buddhist temple.

It is recorded in a Buddhist sutra that a poor beggar girl caught the eye of a king during a hunting trip. He brought her back to his palace and made her his queen. She indeed transformed from a crow into a phoenix in an instant. A poor oil vendor in ancient China unintentionally caught the ball of rolled silk thrown by a noble beauty in her effort to find a spouse, and he

became wealthy overnight. So there is nothing in the world that is really impossible. When the causes and conditions are right, anything is possible!

Plants need soil to grow, but with hydroponics vegetables can develop green shoots and leaves just as well. Today, the sea can be transformed into land, and fields can become part of the ocean. What is impossible in the world? Scientists are doing so much research in laboratories because nothing seems impossible to them. In the life of explorers, accomplishing any mission is also possible.

J. K. Rowling was on welfare, struggling to survive from day to day. Since she published the Harry Potter books, she has now become a multi-billionaire. Milton was blind from a young age, but after his tireless struggle, he became a great poet.

As long as we have perseverance, vision, confidence and wisdom, nothing is impossible. So let's all work hard together!

HOMECOMING

Going home means returning to our origins, essence, or element. For instance, we go back to nature, tradition, the basics, original profession, or our native country. Other forms of homecoming include: leaves returning to their roots, thinking of the fountainhead when we drink water, tracing our ancestry, and finding the way home after a long trip. Repenting our transgressions and purifying ourselves are examples of going back to our original, pure nature.

After the Buddha attained enlightenment under the bodhi tree, he said, "Marvelous! Marvelous! All sentient beings have the wisdom and virtues of Buddha Nature. They just cannot realize it because of their illusions and attachments." This means people continually transmigrate between living and dying and cannot return to their original state of nirvana.

Look at the numerous salmon swimming upstream every fall to spawn. Theirs is a journey of life and death. Every year, the hairy crabs that survive the fishermen's nets return to the sea in droves to breed, going home to extend the life of their species. Poet Gong Zizhen wrote, "The falling red flowers are not without sentiments; they transform into spring soil to nourish the flowers." The withered flower petals in compost become nutrients for the next generation of flowers.

Homecoming is the wish of travelers as they leave home, and people who have lost their way. It is the heart of all mothers waiting for their children to return, and the dream of troops deployed overseas in battle.

Many Chinese poets have written numerous verses on the sentiments of homecoming. Li Bai wrote, "Through the ages, on the battlefield, how many people can actually return?" Su Shi said, "I want to go back to ride the wind, but I fear the heights of the jade palaces in heaven; the cold will be too much to bear." Meng Haoran alluded to coming home in saying, "the threads in the hands of a loving mother, the clothes on the bodies of traveling children, sewing with care and diligence before their departure, and worrying that they will come home late." In the Epoch

of the Three Kingdoms, renowned General Quan Yu once bemoaned, "While my body is in the Cao camp, my heart is with the Han." His desire to go home was a display of his righteousness and genuine sentiments.

People today are lost in the dust and agitation of the external world. They have lost their innate true heart. Chan Master Zhaozhou started off on his journey to learn at the age of eighty, only to discover upon his return home that he had wasted shoe money on the trip. Ming Dynasty's Venerable Master Hanshan once lamented, "The old dusty road is long. Why do we travel to another town? Turning my head, only to see the mountain back home is very far, and the empty clouds in the setting sun fill my eyes." People pursue something outside, only to end up lingering in "a foreign land." After going down the wrong path for many miles, they realize that the treasure they have been eagerly chasing after is actually right inside their hearts.

Homecoming should be joyous and stem from the desire to be home. After we set our goal, we should never hesitate to proceed or stumble on our way. It takes courage to come to terms with the mistake of being lost. So we must have faith and consider it a matter of course. In addition, we need clear direction and the perseverance to never look back in our endeavors.

Self-reflection is a part of homecoming. External causes, conditions, and the guidance of benevolent friends are also necessary. As the saying goes, "Turn your head, and there is the shore." This means "repent, and liberation is at hand." People in business ventures should go back to their original profession if things are not going well. Practitioners need to return to their initial resolve when faced with setbacks. As for travelers, go home quickly to the arms of your mother!

VALUE PROFESSIONALISM

In today's society, more and more people recognize the need to value professionalism. Those who want to practice medicine must study the profession in a medical school. People who want to be teachers must study education in a college. The same is true for plumbing, electronics, electronic appliances, and air-conditioning professionals. Even in the cooking profession, there is a broad spectrum of professional cooks who specialize in the preparation of different foods.

In the past, we probably only needed the help of one person, even if we wanted to build a house. This person might have been able to design, draft, and actually build with mortar and timber all by himself. Now, within the construction profession there are experts in each trade. Even artists specialize in their own field of interest such as stills, animals, or portraits. We have entered the age where professionalism is valued and the time of the one-man band has been phased out. By valuing professionalism, the construction of society improves, and its development is harmonized.

Once, a raftsman was carrying a philosopher down a rapid river. The philosopher asked the raftsman, "Do you understand history?" The raftsman replied, "No." The philosopher criticized him, "Then you have already lost half of life!" He pressed further, "You ever study mathematics?" The raftsman answered, "No." The philosopher again criticized him, "Then you have lost more than half of life!" Just as he finished saying this, a giant wave overturned the raft and both of them fell into the water. The raftsman asked the philosopher, "Do you know how to swim?" The philosopher exclaimed, "No!" With much sympathy, the raftsman said, "Then you are going to lose your whole life!"

There is a saying, "Jack of all trades, master of none." This is indeed true. How is it possible for anyone to learn so many skills and professions within several decades of one's life? Therefore, we are only able to explore in depth our own interest, according to our needs. The leaders of individual professions should value professionalism by not expecting everyone to be good at everything. Parents should not demand that their children learn every

skill and type of sports. It is invaluable if their children are able to be an expert in one particular profession. Such outdated parental thinking is no longer in tune with the needs of modern society. Hopefully, everyone in the modern world values professionalism, and stays in tune with the changing times.

THE FAMILY TREASURE CHEST

Would you like a family treasure chest with a treasure that keeps multiplying? Here are some suggestions.

I. Treasure chest of spirit and action

1. Diligence - Being diligent and hardworking is the way to wealth. Money does not flow in with the tide without reason. Even when it does, we still need to get up early in the morning when the tide is high to pick it up.

2. Frugality - Resources are hard to come by. By being frugal, we can gain wealth.

3. Cherish what we have - Cherishing our merits is cherishing our possessions. We can make them last longer by taking care of them. This is intangible wealth.

4. Planning - As the saying goes, "One does not become poor from getting clothed and fed, but poor economics can put us into poverty for life." When we plan and make a budget, we can put our finances in order. By making ends meet and finding new sources of income, we can eventually gain wealth.

II. Treasure chest of family matters

1. People have their careers - Each adult should have his or her own career.

2. Homemakers have their work - Every homemaker works at home and is also a professional.

3. Elders' role after retirement - Even though family elders retire, they have reached the peak of maturity and wisdom, so they should continue to contribute.

4. The young combine work with studies - Independence is the catchword for many young people today. Young people should care more about household matters and family finances and learn to understand the difficulties of life. Then they will be successful in the future.

III. Treasure chest of the land

1. Utilization of the family land - When a family owns land, it should be cultivated. When we plant and cultivate in spring and

summer, we can harvest in fall and store the crops in winter.

2. Fruit trees in the backyard - When possible, grow a few fruit trees in the backyard. As they blossom and bear fruit, they liven up and nourish the household.

3. Garden in the front yard - Add greenery to the front yard. Plant flowers and shrubs to improve the appeal of the home. Then even the neighbors will be proud.

4. Basement office - The family basement can be used for more than watching television. It can be used as an office for a home-run business, which can earn income for the household.

IV. Treasure chest of mind and body

1. Wisdom - Wisdom is wealth, and it is worth much more than labor.

2. Compassionate eyes and helping hands - Planting seeds of charity may appear to benefit others only. In reality, they benefit us most.

3. Mindfulness and skillfulness - We should know ourselves well and with skillful means provide others with good causes and conditions, helping them to succeed.

4. Form good affinity with kind words - Help others with kind words and encouragement, and make good connections with them.

Our body is a treasure chest in itself. It should be cared for with good nutrition, exercise, and sleep. We have endless treasure if we make good use of our six senses. Similarly, we have a treasure chest in our family, because there is treasure in its people, places, and things. We just need to make good use of them.

WHEN WORRY COMES

Are we worried? Of course we are! When we talk about our health, we are worried. When we feel concerned about financial gains and losses, we become worried. When we are apprehensive about the future, we are distressed. These worries stem from negativity.

When we have too much land and not enough resources to make use of every acre, we are worried. When we have too many houses and cannot fill every one of them, we are concerned. When we have too much money and do not know how to properly invest it, we are troubled. When we build relationships with too many people and don't know how to deal with them effectively, we are frustrated. These worries originate from having too much.

How can we lead a carefree life if we worry when there is too much or too little? What exactly is worry? Most ordinary people do not really know! We are always worried about one thing or another. Worry is "ignorance." When we lack clear understanding, we are worried. Worry is like bad company; when it comes, all our good friends leave at once. It is like a devastating typhoon or hurricane that wreaks havoc in our minds. Although worry is without shape or form, it is like a rope that binds us tightly.

Where does worry come from? Sorrow and grief are worries, and so are hatred and jealousy. Things that we like or dislike can also cause worry. When we look closely, we will find them hidden deep in our minds. It is from there that every one of our worries arises, leaving us restless day and night.

We become annoyed when we hear words that grate on our ears, or see an action that we are uncomfortable with. We have worries because we care too much about material gains and losses. We worry about matters that concern us directly and indirectly, such as when our children do not behave properly, cannot get into a good school, or have yet to get married. Even the rise and fall of the stock market can bring us worry.

We know that all our worries come from the "I" in us. Although we are competent enough to deal with worldly affairs, we feel small, powerless, and weak when we confront our own

worries. Once a man had some worries, so he asked a Chan master to offer him a solution—a way to clear his mind of all defilements. Instead of offering him an answer, the master asked, "Where are your worries?" We are, in fact, our own worries! They are embedded in our minds, and we are the only ones who have the power to eradicate them. Undoubtedly, fame, fortune, greed, anger, having and lacking can bring worry, but if we can set aside all these causes, we will be very far away from any kind of worry.

Someone once asked Winston Churchill about his worries. Humorously, the former British Prime Minister replied, "Whenever I am worried, I remember the words of a dying man who said that although half of his life was spent on worrying about things they never happened."

If we spend most of our days worrying about ourselves, we will certainly be preoccupied. However, if we forget ourselves and think selflessly about our country, society, fellow citizens, our jobs and service to others, we will live without worry and have infinite joy in our lives.

REGRET

Once there was a young scholar who failed the imperial exam and lived in abject poverty. A few years later, he passed with flying colors and earned a high official position in the imperial court. At that point, his neighbors regretted not having helped when he was down and out. Similarly, a poor family with many children never received a word of comfort from anyone when they did not have enough to eat or warm clothes to wear. When the children grew up and became successful, their former neighbors regretted not having provided assistance because then they could have shared in the glory.

We may watch a farmer scrimp and save, planting seeds in the fields, while we spend and enjoy life. By the time harvest comes, we may be left with nothing. Others learn hard as we slack off, unwilling to learn and work. We may even laugh at them for foolishly studying so hard. When they succeed and we do not make any progress, we will only be left with regret.

There are many things in life that we may regret. Sages in the past often reminded us, "If we do not study from our teachers while we are with them, or if we fail to learn from the wise when we meet them, what is the use of regret after we part?" Similarly, if we do not show filial piety and take care of our parents when they are with us, after they pass away we will no longer have the opportunity to do so, even if we want to. When people are disloyal to their superiors, they may live to regret it when they face difficulties with their jobs. When we fail to take the opportunity to support a good cause or to donate money to charity, regret does not help us when the chance or our money is gone. If we do not believe in the law of cause and effect and only learn to regret by tasting the bitter fruit of retribution, it does not improve our situation. Furthermore, if we do not cultivate the path of Buddhahood when we should, it will be too late to regret when our life ends!

When we do not have the foresight to plan ahead, we only have regrets and afterwards suffer the consequences. Therefore, the wise always anticipate the results of their actions and act with a clear conscience, so there will be no regrets in the future. We

should have no regrets in what we say and do. Buddhism teaches that a person with attachments, anger, suspicion, greed, and indecisiveness will certainly have regrets. On the other hand, a courageous, righteous, and kind person will gain the sympathy of others if he or she does something wrong and regrets it.

Once a thirteen-year-old boy wrote to President Cleveland, "Dear President, I have done something wrong against the nation. I acted in an unconscionable way by using a cancelled stamp. I am filled with regrets, and I am willing to pay it back now. Mr. President, please pardon me." The letter is filled with innocence and love. It was saved and has become one of the most valued letters in the White House.

It is important that we perform good deeds in daily life, and not bad deeds that we will regret later. We should leave behind benevolence and innocence for people in the world; never regrets or remorse.

ONE MINUTE

How long is a minute? It can be very short or very long. One minute is all the difference between glory and shame, life and death, or gain and loss.

Some people do not take an hour, a day, a year or even a lifetime seriously, let alone a minute. Living in confusion and delusion, they let life go by. Other people take a minute very seriously as they race with time, fighting daily for each second and minute. For instance, students rush to school every morning not wanting to be late. Government employees and factory workers who have to sign in or punch a card also take a minute very seriously. In international tournaments, the winning teams' years of hard work are sometimes left to the last minute of the game. There are diligent people who, at the last minute, are able to turn failure into success.

Some people know how to use time well. They can memorize an idiom or learn a new word in a minute. They may use a minute to give others a smile, to shake their hands, or to just say hello. The minute they spend may affect their lives in a major way and gain much for their future. Some people can resolve major issues for their country, society, or organization in one minute. However, others may spend a year or a whole lifetime and still not find a solution to their personal problems. Consequently, a minute or a hundred years makes no difference to them.

One minute can indeed make a huge difference. A doctor can revive a life, a lifeguard can rescue someone from drowning, and a firefighter can save a victim in less than a minute. Before a fire can spread, one minute is all it takes to put it out. For people who are always tardy, they may be one minute late for a train or plane and miss an important appointment. In addition, during earthquakes and other disasters, where life and death is a matter of a moment, one minute is indeed crucial.

In gaining a minute, we may accomplish something major. However, a minute can also ruin a life. For instance, in trying to be a minute early, some motorists may run a red light and speed across the intersection, resulting in a wreck and a fatality.

When there are emergencies in life, we need to fight for each minute, because a minute gained may save lives and relieve suffering. However, if we are too calculating about one minute, refusing to give even one step, the consequences can also be dire. Therefore, we say, "Don't rush, don't rush! Safety first!" Because even though it is a minute, we still have to be clear about the consequences.

Time is life. Though we may live for decades, the seconds and minutes never stop. "Time shoots by like an arrow, as the sun and moon rise and set like the weaver's shuttle." Some people like to talk incessantly. Not only are they wasting their own lives but also that of others.

There are people who do not cherish time. When they see others busy at work, they ask, "Please give me a minute. I have three questions to ask you." Or, "I have a friend who wants to see you. Please give him a minute." How can three questions be answered in a minute? Is one minute enough to deal with a guest?

Life hinges on a breath, and life and death is only a matter between seconds and minutes. So is a minute long or short? The length of time depends on how we use it. When gain, loss, glory, shame, success and failure are involved, we cannot afford to ignore one minute!

PARALYSIS

When functions of the body degenerate or muscles lose their flexibility and sensitivity, numbness sets in and the person is paralyzed. While physical paralysis is the result of serious diseases, if our minds cease to be compassionate about the suffering of the world and have no wisdom to help resolve other's problems, we have mental paralysis.

When politicians are shameless, their callousness and lack of scruples are signs of character paralysis. Some people have no passion for work; others speak without rhyme or reason. They are numb to what they do as well as to their relationships with others. Some people who suffer from illness may use painkillers to dull the pain. However, other people drink to drown their sorrows, seeking to numb their senses momentarily. Now, many young people do drugs, indulge in substance abuse, and linger in arcades. They are paralyzing both their minds and character.

There are other signs of paralysis in society. The media choose to report sensationalism and not positive news. Many people who lack ethics refuse to support social causes, do not know the importance of hard work, and choose to degenerate in life. Society loses morality and integrity, and the justice system often fails its people. This is a paralysis of ethics in society.

However, the national spirit of a country should never be paralyzed! We need to wake up the social spirit, because if no one has self-awareness or is awakened to the need to strive and progress, then every member in society will be paralyzed, dragging the nation down with them. While it is the responsibility of individual members to have self-realization, the government, through appropriate legislation, must also assist those momentarily confused and lost. Many countries in the world have strict laws regarding illegal drug possession and trafficking. However, they should also think of ways to control places such as clubs and rave parties, where the younger generation may degenerate into self-indulgence.

To awaken people from paralysis, we need education, religion, and appropriate recreation. A country's leaders should set

examples for the public by befriending the benevolent and being involved with religious organizations, charities, education, and sports clubs. As members of the community follow suit, social trends can be changed.

Physical paralysis can be cured with physiotherapy and medical equipment. Those with mental and spiritual paralysis should wake up in time to change their situation. If they are determined to turn themselves around or rehabilitate themselves, they can recover and regain their health over time.

LOOKING FOR TROUBLE

"There is really nothing to worry about except trouble of our own making." To make much ado about nothing is to be anxious over what is groundless and imaginary. Where does worry come from? It is the product of our minds. We are increasingly suspicious of the outside world because we do not recognize its true nature. We are more attached to material possessions because we have lost sight of their insignificance. We are ignorant and deluded because we do not yet understand the true nature of the mind. We are arrogant and conceited because we refuse to respect the achievements of others. Many problems are created because we fail to understand the truth.

Where does trouble come from? It comes from lust and desire. Emperors lost their empires and even their lives because of lewdness and immorality. Generals and soldiers betrayed their countries and sold themselves when they could not resist the seductions of a beautiful spy.

Where does trouble come from? It comes from a person's thirst for fame, fortune, and power. Many politicians and high-ranking officials have lost their hard-earned reputations because of greed and corruption. Due to their shameless solicitation of bribes in the pursuit of self-interest and the commission of fraudulent acts, they trade glory for a prison sentence.

Where does trouble come from? It comes from a person's desire for love, money, worldly attachments, and illusions. We are, indeed, asking for trouble when we take everything too seriously and indulge in wishful thinking. We are looking for trouble when we isolate ourselves and occupy our minds with pettiness. For instance, we may constantly worry about our weight or height.

Where does trouble come from? It comes from the habit of engaging in libelous talk and scandals. It is, indeed, a nuisance for people to spread rumors and listen to gossip. To avoid trouble, we must restrain ourselves in the face of untruths and hearsay. If we can exercise a little caution in what we hear, see or speak, our ears, eyes and mouth will be well guarded, without causing any

problem.

Where does trouble come from? It comes from a distorted sense of competition and comparison. It is common for some people to be competitive throughout their lives, from childhood to old age. They compete with their little playmates for the attention of being the cutest and the smartest. They compare grades and girlfriends with schoolmates to see who has the highest scores and the prettiest girl. For them, competition does not end with maturity and adulthood. They continue to compete and compare every aspect of their lives, including marriage, career, social status, and wealth. Even when they are old and feeble, they fuss about their children and grandchildren, health, longevity, and legacies. No wonder their lives are full of trouble, for they spend every waking moment fussing over and comparing one thing or another.

In reality, our world is full of decay and defilements. We have not only failed to get out of trouble, but have also found ways to stay in it, and continue to look for more. Since all of our problems are self-made, we should learn to solve them ourselves. As the saying goes, "although gossip and scandals are everyday occurrences, disregard them and they will naturally disappear." If we do not want trouble, we must not look for it. We must not give trouble any reason to arise.

FEAR

What do you fear in this world? When we say we are not afraid of ghosts, lions or tigers, it is not so hard to believe. However, do you fear that your conscience will blame you for what you have done? Do you fear karmic retribution? We may have no fear of heaven or earth, but we must fear our own conscience and karmic retribution according to the law of causality.

People fear so many things. Women fear old age, old people fear death, heroes fear sickness, and children fear the dark. Do you have many fears? In reality, people may not fear anything in the world except people. For instance, aren't nitpicking bosses, bureaucratic officers, cheating friends, fierce wives, and alcoholic husbands fearful?

Besides people fearing other people, there are many who are afraid of animals. Some people have phobias of mice, snakes, cockroaches, earthworms, spiders, caterpillars, hornets, etc. The weak-hearted fear everything, whereas very confident people fear nothing. However, parading one's superiority does not mean one is truly strong. There are many things in the world far stronger than people. Are you afraid of fires, floods, and earthquakes? Are you not afraid when a couple of ghosts stand before you?

Through the ages, Confucianists encouraged scholars to have respect for the heavens and fear of deities. Buddhism teaches devotees to fear karmic power and the law of causality. Even bodhisattvas fear causes. The Buddha himself was afraid of "worms on the lion's body," meaning those who harm the Dharma while feeding off of it. Therefore, the truth fears gossip, gossip fears the wise, ignorance fears wisdom, and the wicked fear the righteous.

Everything in the world has its own enemy, and every animal or plant has its nemesis. For instance, mice fear cats, cats fear dogs, elephants fear mice, frogs fear snakes, snakes fear centipedes, centipedes fear chickens, trees fear worms, and computers fear hackers.

Fear is not the monopoly of the weak. Sometimes the most powerful countries fear invasion, the strongest organizations are afraid of infighting, and prodigal children, and the closest of sib-

lings fear backbiting. In addition, thieves fear the police, criminals the law, and drivers fear traffic jams. Travelers fear getting lost, and seafarers are afraid of losing their bearing.

The following quotations refer to the universal emotion of fear: "People fear pain and suffering, while trees fear being stripped of their bark and uprooted." "Have no fear of being unemployed, but fear that your skills are not good enough." "Have no fear of suffering when young, but fear poverty when old." "People should fear laziness most, because lazy people never succeed." Humble Table, Wise Fare says, "Lazy people lose their fortune and merits; diligent people gain merits."

People used to criticize henpecked men as good for nothing. In reality, men who are afraid of their wives are often good husbands. What is not good about their fear?

CAPABILITIES

Everything in the world has its own capabilities. When its capabilities are good, its value is high, and vice versa.

The Buddha said, "All sentient beings have Buddha Nature." This means all sentient beings have the same natural capabilities. However, because of differences in growth, their level of diligence, and other external causes and conditions, people's knowledge and achievements are different. Likewise, products are either superior or inferior due to differences in materials and the manufacturing process. It is like starting a race from the same line. After the race starts, because of individual capabilities, the results will not be the same.

We may be able to buy a plain kitchen knife for a few dollars, but if we want a really good one it may cost more than a hundred. Similarly, an average car may cost several thousand dollars, but a superior one will cost significantly more. So the value of a product is directly affected by its capabilities.

Besides the capabilities of a thing, we also have to consider its functions. Land in the city may cost hundreds of thousands of dollars per square foot, but farmland in the countryside only costs a fraction of that amount per acre. This also applies to people. Top movie stars often make millions of dollars a month, while some people cannot find a job and support themselves. Objects such as computers, cameras, photocopiers, and cell phones all vary in price because of their different functions.

Whether we are shopping for material goods, food, gas or medicine, there are many product grades and thus differences in price. Because their functions vary, so do the prices. Sometimes when a person's or object's functions are too good, it brings trouble. As the saying goes, "The capable have more work." Life is harder for those with more and better capabilities. And if people are very good at what they do, they will be the target of envy and criticism. The more beautifully that flowers bloom, the more quickly they are picked. Likewise, a tree that grows big and tall will be chopped down. Therefore, people with capabilities must be able to withstand the pressures of the world. The more pressure

and criticism a person can bear, the more valuable and accomplished he or she is because of his or her outstanding capabilities. Buddhism teaches, "The four elements are empty." This means all beings and phenomena are made of the four elements of earth, water, fire and air, and therefore possess all of their different characteristics. We should be like the good earth and nurture and embrace all beings; we should be like water and moisturize all beings and flow comfortably wherever we go. We should be like fire and create civilization and warmth in the world; we should be like gentle breezes, at ease anywhere and spreading seeds for life to grow.

We should foster and improve our capabilities. We should cultivate righteousness, loyalty, benevolence, honesty, loving-kindness, peacefulness, and humility. We should develop the treasure within our capabilities, and bring into full play the value of our humanity.

ONE

A myriad of things exist in the universe, but none of them is the one and only; so we can appreciate all their different shapes and sizes. Luckily, there is only one Earth; otherwise, we would worry about a possible collision.

In Chinese history, there were the five regions of the Spring and Autumn Epoch, the seven warlords of the Warring States, the Three Kingdoms, the Five Nomadic Tribes, and Sixteen States. They fought endlessly, taking the "one" apart. But if there had only been one China, eventually there would have been peace. Together, the population of China and Taiwan is more than 1.3 billion today. We should unite in heart like a massive army in our effort to repay our country, so that it can be strong.

When there is one father and one mother in a family, there should be peace in life. However, children may shirk the responsibility of caring for their aging parents, even when there are many of them. They tend to look to other siblings to shoulder the burden. Sometimes after parents pass away, siblings fight over the family fortune, even though they are so closely related. Therefore, having many children does not necessarily spell good fortune.

If there is only one roadway, we will not be distracted by a sidetrack. Ocean routes and airport runways are singularly designed to minimize mistakes and reduce accidents. In the world of commerce, an individual business may be the leader of the pack. However, there is often vicious competition. If there is a center or leadership amidst this colorful variety, everyone can conduct business in peace.

A single child gets all the love and attention of the parents. Though it is said that a single tree does not make a forest, trees in the woods do not reject one another but support each other instead. "Ten thousand peach blossoms come from one root." That is what Chinese Taoists taught on how one becomes two, two becomes four, and four becomes all phenomena. Buddhism also teaches "All dharma realms are in one mind." "One" is the foundation.

Any one of our ten fingers has little or no power, but when they form a fist, there is strength. So we should not reject the "many." They only need to join together as one! As long as we cooperate, we can unite to become one force. The sun brings us warmth, and the moon gives us cool light. However, in our one universe, thousands of stars in the sky light our lives with beauty.

One useful phrase is enough if it benefits many, because a thousand useless sentences are not helpful to even one person. We may have two eyes, but a sculptor closes one eye, using only the other one to craft a piece of art, because this is more precise. We only have one mouth to rely on for eating in order to get enough nutrition to live.

Pines and bamboo are much admired because they tend to be singular and straight, not leaning this way or that. People with endless desires open one company and want to establish a second and a third branch. These so-called chain stores will be in trouble when the economy is not doing well as they may fall like dominoes, with disastrous consequences. A temple may have many branches, but they are all under the same Buddha and uphold one set of precepts. When unity is strength, "one" is not little and "many" is also one. So what is wrong in being "one?" We have five toes on one foot that do not separate or reject one another, and thus they can be viewed as one.

There is a saying, "Have no fear of a tiger with three mouths; only fear people who have two minds." If we are single-minded in what we do, we have nothing to be afraid of, because all dharmas lead to one. When we transform all phenomena in the world into "one," like a compassionate heart, a benevolent practice and a respectful mind, then there will be peace in the world. All things in the world that are separate will eventually unite, and all matters united will break apart someday. We can only hope that our society, country, and race can stay together, or unite if they are apart. The world will be truly beautiful then.

Glossary

Agama Sutras: Also known as the *Nikayas* in the Pali Canon, they include the *Long Discourses*, the *Middle Length Discourses*, the *Connected Discourses*, and the *Gradual Discourses of the Buddha*.

Alaya-vijnana: Literally "storehouse of consciousness." Regarded in the Yogacara or Mind-Only school of the Mahayana tradition as the repository of the essential consciousness of everything that exists. It contains the karmic seeds of individual lives, which in turn give rise to new mental activity. Sometimes also referred to as alaya consciousness or the eighth consciousness.

Amitabha Buddha: The Buddha of the Western Pure Land, also known as the Buddha of Infinite Light, Amita Buddha and Amitayus Buddha, vowed to prepare a purified realm for all those who desired to be reborn in it. Those who recite his name and perform wholesome deeds will be reborn in his Pure Land.

Asceticism: Skt. "dhuta," which means to eliminate afflictions and sufferings, to cultivate the purification of the mind and the body, and to abandon greedy desires.

Avalokitesvera: Literally, "He who hears the sounds of the world." In Mahayana Buddhism, Avalokitesvara is known as the Bodhisattva of Compassion. He can manifest himself in any form necessary in order to help any being. He is considered one of the great bodhisattvas in Mahayana Buddhism. In China, he is well-known as "Guan Yin."

Bodhi: Enlightenment. In the state of enlightenment, one is awakened to the true nature of oneself, the Buddha Nature.

Bodhi Mind: Skt. "bodhicitta," the mind seeking to attain enlightenment.

Bodhisattva: "Enlighening being," refers to anyone who seeks Buddhahood and vows to liberate all sentient beings.

Bodhisattva path: Skt. "Bodhisattva-carya," indicating the cultivation of the bodhisattvas in Mahayana Buddhism. One on the bodhisattva path seeks to attain Buddhahood and liberate all sentient beings through the practice of the six perfections.

Buddha: Literally, "awakened one." When "the Buddha" is used, it usually refers to the historical Buddha, Sakyamuni Buddha.

Buddha Nature: The inherent nature that exists in all beings. It is the capability to attain Buddhahood.

Bodhidharma: The founder of the Chan School in Chinese Buddhism.

Buddhism: Founded by Sakyamuni Buddha around 2,500 years ago, its basic doctrines include the Three Dharma Seals, the Four Noble Truths, the Noble Eightfold Path, the Twelve Links of Dependent Origination, the six perfections, and the concepts of impermanence and emptiness. It has long been a popular religion in South, Central and East Asia and is currently growing in the West.

Chan: The Chinese transliteration of the Sanskrit term "dhyana, " meditation.

Chan Buddhism: A school of Buddhism that emphasizes enlightenment through deep concentration, meditation, and internal cultivation. Practicing Chan Buddhism does not rely upon intellectual reasoning, analysis of doctrine, or academic studies, but instead, relies upon a profound inner concentration that can reveal and illuminate one's true nature. (Chan in Japan is called "Zen".)

Confucianism: The philosophy named after Confucius. It was the

official philosophy of China, established in the third century B.C.E.

Confucianism's "Three Bonds and Five Constant Virtues": The three mainstays of social order: the relationships of ruler-subject, father-child and husband-wife. Adding the relationships between brothers and between friends to the three bonds forms the five main principles of social order in Confucianism.

Confucius: (551-479 B.C.E) In Chinese, "Kungzi." He was an early Chinese moral philosopher. Founder of the philosophy later known as Confucianism.

Cultivation: Synonymous with "practice." Cultivation is the training of heart and mind in generosity, virtue, calmness, wisdom, etc.

Dharma: With a capital "D": 1) the ultimate truth, and 2) the teachings of the Buddha. When the Dharma is applied or practiced in life, it is 3) righteousness or virtues. With a lower case "d": 4) anything that can be thought of, experienced, or named; close in meaning to "phenomena."

Dharma joy: The joy that arises in the mind after listening to or learning the Buddha's teachings.

Dharmapada Sutra: *Sutra on the Treasury of Truth*. Ch. *Faju Jing*. Also known as *The Word of Truth, The Treasury of Truth*, or *The Treasures of the Truth*.

Diamond Sutra: The *Vajracchedika Prajna Paramita Sutra*. The *Diamond Sutra* sets forth the doctrine of emptiness and the perfection of wisdom. It is so named because the perfection of wisdom cuts like a diamond through delusion.

Ekottara-Agama Sutra: *"Gradual Discourses of the Buddha."*

Ch. "*Zeng Yi Ahan Jing*, " in Pali "*Anguttara Nikaya*." It contains 52 fascicles and 472 sutras. Compared with other *Agama Sutra*, it is the most recent, and it embraces the Mahayana philosophy. It was named this because the Buddha gradually discourses upon the methods of practice, from one kind to eleven kinds of practice.

Emptiness: Skt. "sunyata." A fundamental Buddhist concept, also known as non-substantiality or relativity, meaning all phenomena have no fixed or independent nature. In Buddhism, it can be divided into two categories: 1) associated with individuals and called "non-substantiality of persons," 2) associated with phenomena and called "non-substantiality of dharmas." Therefore, the concept of emptiness is related to dependent origination and impermanence.

Four Embracing Virtues and Six Perfections: The four embracing virtues are generosity, kind words, conduct beneficial to others, and cooperation with and adapation of oneself to others. The six "perfections" practiced by enlightened beings are generosity, upholding the precepts, patience, diligence, meditation, and wisdom.

Heart Sutra: One of the most important sutras in Mahayana Buddhism. It is regarded as the essence of Buddhist teachings and is chanted daily in communities all over the world.

Journey to the West: A famous Chinese classical novel.

Ksitigarbha Bodhisattva: One of the great bodhisattvas of Mahayana Buddhism. Ksitigarbha Bodhisattva vowed to remain in hell until all sentient beings are released from it.

Lotus Sutra: This sutra is one of the most important sutras in Mahayana Buddhism. The major emphasis in this sutra is the concept of the integration of the vehicles of the sravaks and

pratyekabuddhas and that of the bodhisattvas into the one Buddha vehicle.

Maharatnakuta Sutra: *"Collection of Great Treasures."* Ch. *Da Baoji Jing.* The title refers to the accumulation of great Dharma treasures and innumerable methods. This sutra emphasizes the bodhisattvas' cultivation methods and records the Buddha's prediction of their progress in attaining Buddhahood. The methods include the teachings and practices of emptiness, and the Pure Land, and Esoteric schools.

Mahayana: Literally, "The Great Vehicle." One of the two main traditions of Buddhism; the other is Theravada. Mahayana Buddhism stresses that helping all sentient beings attain enlightenment is as important as self-liberation.

Medicine Buddha's World of Pure Crystal: The Medicine Buddha is the Buddha of healing. He presides over the Eastern Pure Land.

Mencius: Second most important Confucian philosopher.

Merit: The blessings of wealth, health, intelligence, etc., which are accrued through virtuous conduct and benefiting others.

Monk Budai: "Cloth-bag" monk, an erratic monk in the early tenth century. He was noted for his shoulder bag and was often depicted as a joyful monk.

Mount Putuo: One of the four most famous mountains in China, located in Zhejiang Province. It is considered the sacred mountain of Avalokitesvara Bodhisattva.

Mount Tai: A famous mountain located in Shandong Province, China.

One Hundred Parables Sutra: Translated by Gunavrddhi in the late fifth century. It uses parables to explain the Dharma.

Parinirvana: A synonym for "nirvana." It is the state of having completed all merits and perfections and eliminated all unwholesomeness. Usually, it is used to refer to the time when the Buddha physically passed away.

Patriarch: In Buddhism, the founder of a school and his successors in the transmission of the teaching.

Prajna: Literally, "wisdom." As the highest form of wisdom, prajna is the wisdom of insight into "emptiness," which is the true nature of all phenomena. The realization of prajna also implies the attainment of enlightenment, and is in this sense one of the six paramitas or "perfections" of the bodhisattva path. Sometimes referred to by the compound term, prajna-wisdom.

Pratyekabuddha: literally, "solitary awakened one." One who attains enlightenment on his own, without having heard the teachings of a Buddha.

Preface of Lan Ting Collection: A literacy piece by Wang Xizhi, who is one of the most famous Chinese calligraphers. The piece is deemed to be one of the best examples of the running script style of Chinese calligraphy.

Sakyamuni Buddha: (581 - 501 B.C.E.) The historical founder of Buddhism He was born the Prince of Kapilavastu, son of King Suddhodana. At the age of twenty-nine, he left the royal palace and his family to search for the meaning of existence. At the age of thirty-five, he attained enlightenment under the bodhi tree. He then spent the next forty-five years expounding his teachings, which include the Four Noble Truths, the Eightfold Path, the Law of Cause and Effect, and Dependent Origination. At age eighty, he entered the state of parinirvana.

Samadhi: A deep state of meditative concentration. A state in which the mind is concentrated in a one-pointed focus and all mental activities are calmed. In samadhi, one is free from all distractions, thereby entering a state of inner serenity.

Samyutagama Sutra: *"Connected Discourses of the Buddha."* Ch. *"Zhong Ahan Jing;"* in Pali *"Samyutta Nikaya."* It is named this because those taught by the Buddha include bhiksus, bhiksunis, upaskas, upasikas, and heavenly beings; the teachings also include several subjects such as the Four Noble Truths, the Noble Eightfold Path, and Dependent Origination.

Sravaka: Literally, "hearer." It refers to one who has attained enlightenment after listening to the Buddha's teachings.

Sutra: Literally, "threaded together." The discourses directly taught by the Buddha.

Sutra of the Forty-two Sections: The first sutra translated into Chinese, completed by Kasyapamatanga and Zhu Falan. The content is concise and explains the basic doctrines of early Buddhism; mainly the explanations of the fruits of monastic attainment, the various wholesome and unwholesome karma, the awakening of the mind, the abandonment of desires, the concept of impermanence, and the important meaning of becoming a monastic and of following the path.

Tang Journal of the Western Region: Completed by the Tang Dynasty pilgrim Xuanzhuang in A.D. 646-8.

Tripitaka: Literally, "Three Baskets." The Buddhist canon in three categories: the sutras (teachings of the Buddha), the vinayas (precepts and rules), and the abhidharma (commentary on the Buddha's teachings).

Western Pure Land: Amitabha Buddha's Pure Land which is

located hundreds of thousands of millions of Buddha-land to the west of our Saha world. The Western Pure Land is purified and perfected through Amitabha Buddha's fulfillment of vows and practices.

Yogacara School of Buddhism: One school of Mahayana Buddhism; also known as the Mind-Only School (Vijnanavada). It was founded by Maitreyanatha between the fourth and fifth centuries, and emphasizes the teachings of the *Commentary on the Stages of Yogacara Practitioners (Yogacarabhumi)*.